Ross Edward Percifield II

Diamonds
in the
Rough

A Treasury of 20th Century
Romantic Verse

authorHOUSE®

AuthorHouse™
1663 Liberty Drive
Bloomington, IN 47403
www.authorhouse.com
Phone: 1 (800) 839-8640

Published by AuthorHouse 05/11/2016

ISBN: 978-1-5246-0832-3 (sc)
ISBN: 978-1-5246-0831-6 (e)

Library of Congress Control Number: 2016907644

Print information available on the last page.

For previous copyrights of:

Summerwintertime	*Across Time And Space*
On Man's Eternal Battle	*Evening's Storm*
The Flame	*Nightscape*
My Love For You	*Death Of A Sun*
And Dark Clouds Blew In	*To Winter*
Glory	*Raindrops Fall*
Hot For You	*So Divine*
The Pearl	*Poetic Adoration*
The Candle	*Morning Glory*
Emerald Sleeves	*My Desire*
A Literal Litany	*Bright Star*
Mere Words	*North Wind*
Song Of The Fairy	*Love Songs Immortal*
…see individual poems.	

This book presented to:

By:

_____ Date:_____

This is a Limited First Edition Copy

Contents

BONUS SECTION

A WORD FROM THE AUTHOR

Ever since I was a boy of about fifteen and first began setting my pen to paper to express the deep, new stirrings within my heart and mind I have been in great awe of that wonderful Force that moves inside of me that I have always called poetic inspiration. To create poetry is to sing your heart's own song, paint a grammatical portrait of your emotions, to play a most melodious musical instrument . . . shine a bright beacon on the mirror which reflects your life's deepest secrets and passions . . . that others might also experience and enjoy. Over the years I have come to realize that the fire that drives me to create is the Force, while the verses I set down are merely the result and evidence of the acting of that Force. And, I have grown to know this Force on a personal basis, for, it is our Heavenly Father Jesus Christ, who drives my pen. It is He who has graced me with the experiences and feelings to write about, and the ability and opportunity to do so.
Poetry is a gift. It is a gift, from my God to me.
It is a gift, from me to you.
And, your gift to me . . . your enjoyment!

"Poeta nascitur, non fit…"
A Poet is born, not made

PREFACE TO THE LIMITED EDITION

With the hope you might better appreciate
the little book you now hold in your hands,
I believe it is important for you to know something
of its conception, growth, and how it has evolved
through various stages over the last six years
into the book now presented for your enjoyment.
From the beginning of my efforts to compile a
collection of my poems to be presented to the public
(in 1991, while I was living in Alaska,) this has remained,
predominantly, a self-publishing effort. While I have
investigated other avenues of accomplishing this goal
(independent publishers, subsidy publishing, etc.,) I have
always ended up feeling I had better accomplish this
project entirely through my own efforts. Hence, in
every way except printing and binding, from concep-
tion, compilation, typesetting and formatting; selection
of printer and payment for production; obtainment
of copyright and Library Of Congress Catalog Card
Number; cover design and any graphics, artwork or
photography; and, all marketing and distribution, has
remained the sole responsibility of the Author.
This has, therefore, its advantages, as well as
disadvantages. I have not had the luxury, (or benefit) of
consultation with or criticism from an Editor or Pub-
lisher in the business of producing a book in this genre,
nor of their expertise or means at their disposal. The"Project,"
necessarily, has taken about six years to complete. Just now, as I

have overcome the highest hurdle on the path toward realizing my dream (coming up with the substantial funds necessary to finance this endeavor) and I am in the process of preparing a final manuscript, I am filled with a wonderful mixture of emotions. Of course there is joy and excitement to know that I may soon realize my dream. But, I am now also filled with a quantity of fear and apprehension. Even as I write these words and consider one last time what will be the title, contents, and "theme" of my manuscript, I am attempting to mitigate questions and doubts: How will my book be received by the general public? Can I bear it if it is not well received? Will I be perceived as a vain fool with no real talent or "gift" and end up with a garage full of unsold books gathering dust, and a financial loss of several thousands of dollars? These and other questions, leave me uncertain, even at this late date, whether these words will ever be read, or if the poetic creations to accompany them and all the work and hope that has gone into this project will ever come to fruition.

Yet, driven by that unseen Force, moved by my Romantic optimism and reassured by my recollection of all of the positive reactions I have received over the years when I have shared my poetry with friends, acquaintances, and, those who have been the inspiration for the creations themselves, I push on. And, because of all of these things, and more, I am left believing that this is a book that had to be written, that <u>had</u> to be published and presented to the public; that my thirty years of poetic creation and my life's work up to this date was predestined to "suffer the slings and arrows of outrageous fortune." Therefore, the degree of success or failure of the project becomes secondary to the completion of the task itself. The degree or quality of the poetic skill contained herein, or whether others perceive it as a gift from an unseen Force, are relegated a back seat to the Author's belief in that gift, and Force, and the motivation that drives the Author to share these deep feelings and beliefs with the general public.

So, if you are reading this, the project has been completed

and a wonderful dream has been realized. If this is the case, this
Author would like to make the following wish: that you, the
Reader and Critic, might be moved by the verses you discover
within these meager pages or the Inspiration and Force that fueled
the fire that caused their creation; but, more than anything
else, that you find some measure of enjoyment and
happy reading and that you are left with good
feelings when you are done.

December, 1996

WITH SPECIAL THANKS . . .

The Reader might be just a little bit aston-
ished to learn that this little book now held in
your hands has been in the making for more than
thirty years. From the very earliest poems I wrote
when I was a boy of fifteen, through those I com-
posed in the Fall of last year, each has been
created for the time when this collection would be
ready to present to the public. These poems repre-
sent my life's work, up to the present, though
until now they existed only as fragments, uncon-
nected components of a larger body of work.

It could not be until just recently that I was
struck with the realization that this "work" was
sufficiently completed, and the inspiration that
allowed me to conceive of these "fragments" of all
that I have written, extracted from that larger
body of work, polished and assembled to stand as a
separate unit, now providing an example of a thing
being greater than the sum of its individual parts.

Now, as I prepare to ship this manuscript off
to the printer and this amazing process enters its
final stage, I pause to express my sincere appreci-
ation to all those individuals who have assisted me
in so many ways over the life of this project. From
purely technical assistance, to moral support and
encouragement, there are many people I would like
to thank for helping me make a dream become a reality.

Without their help, your hands would grasp
naught but air . . . instead of the volume now held there.

In honor of all of you . . . friends, loved ones, mere acquaintances . . . for your help, support, patience and love . . . I mention your names herein and give you all of my heartfelt thanks!

My Dad, **Ross Edward Percifield** . . . for the peacefulness and strength of spirit and the example you always set . . .

My Mom, **Dorothy Marilyn Percifield** . . . for the passion and sensitivity, and love of the written word . . .

My brothers and sisters:
Stephanie Ann
Mark Lincoln
Kathryn
Martin Lucas

My Dearest Friends, and your families . . . for standing by me during the hard times, as well as the good times, and for giving me the greatest gift of all . . . your Love:
Bill and Donna Briggs Art Portnoff Don "Tiny" Vitelli
Tommy Conway Alan Chris Posich
Elizabeth Shannon Slotten Joey Williams
Judi Nipps Laurel Garcia
Joyce Jakemer Fixler Robert Frensley
Brian Cescolini Jim Foy Robyn O'Neal
Susan Catherine and Audra Blake

April Poretta, for proofing and for your critique of my manuscript

My Loving Lord and Savior, **Jesus Christ** . . . for <u>everything</u>!

THE WORKS

ARRIVAL AND DEPARTURE

Prepare for me

I am coming to you

Greet me

I am here

Embrace me

I am near to you

Hold me tight

I am wanting you

Love me

I am yours

Kiss me

I am leaving you

Remember me

I am gone

ALL THAT GOD HAS BUILT

The Mediterranean breeze
    plays softly with our hair
Telling of the Grace of God
    and His Kingdom where
All is pure and sweet and good
    for all those who are there

As we press this soft sand
    underneath our feet
Don't you wish that we had tasted
    something near as sweet
When we used to live back there
    In that great big town
Where all it seems they ever did
    was tear things down?

When we finally climb
    that lofty mountain peak
Let's stop and look down on the earth
    and realize just how weak
Man must be to throw away
    all that God has built
And have the nerve and lowliness
    to do so without guilt

ODE TO LIFE

The Morning Sun
    Life begins

Birds sing
    and a drop of Dew
        falls from a forgotten leaf
            in the Meadow of my Memory

One streak of radiance
    shoots through a branch
        from whence came
            our falling drop of Dew

This ray
    strikes a single grain of sand
        on which is perched
            a lonely Particle of Time

Oh! Ageless Breath of Life
    tireless one

Stand firm and strong
    Last forever
        And longer

Fill yourself with thoughts of
    Pleasure and do not feel as
        Though you are not what you
            are

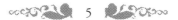

MY SUMMER ROSE

On light and silent little toes
To sprinkle softly, flakes so fine
In creeps first of many snows
Covering all but one lone pine
Under this a rose will keep
And wait for Spring, while, in her sleep
She dreams of rays, so soft and warm
As Blue Jays and other nice things take form
The snow begins to melt and grass pops up
All around
If one had walked to where she stood
He would have surely found
A feeling of warmth deep in his heart
For, in the ground where she waited so long
To put forth her ware
You may now see why the tree above
Sheltered her with such care
She's my Summer Rose, my Winter Wine
No matter where she goes, she's mine

DEW DROPS

As silent little stars
Twinkle toward their daytime bed
And swiftly pass beyond our eyes
Before the coming red
Colors that are not
Hop aboard the train
And depart as swift as did
The gentle little rain

ENDLESS QUEST

Whether bird, squirrel, or fragrant flower
In crowded city or lonely tower
Whether snow, wind, or driving rain
On mountainside or tranquil plain
A diamond, emerald or flawless pearl
The purest gem adorning a little girl
It matters not what time or place
For, each alone has a special grace
While I sit and dream, in meditation
It hits me, a thing I call "inspiration"
It is always there, and awaits me, now
and again
If I look close and wait with steady pen
I'll catch the moment that's so right
If I'll sit still as birds take flight
And let the ink flow free and strong
It will spill the words to sing my song
So sweet and pure with notes so clear
And when I have them, so all may hear
I climb to highest peak and look up to the sky
Gather all my strength and in one great cry
Hurl the words out from myself and into space
Then stand and wait for what is, in this case
A change of ways for man and child
To say they've heard my song and smiled
Which means they understand and in some way
Will be better off from this very day

Then came the answer from far above
As skies parted there soared a dove
Right through the clouds and to my ear
And whispered the news I waited to hear
I now sing my song and teach the rest
The noble reason for my endless quest:
To spread faith and brotherhood and love
Bestowed on us all by a great God above

AS EASY AS THE ABC'S

A good person will
B a kind, wise one, who will
C that there are others who
D zerve the same consideration and
E qual treatment as themselves and
F we all understood this life would be
    wonderful.
G!
H would not be used as often to spell
    "Hate."
I wish that people would be happy
    And friendly.
J birds would sing and be gay and
    Things would be O.
K.
L would be much less crowded and I
M sure Heaven would be much more populated
N abling God to leave more happy people
    Here on Earth.
O, but to think of a whole world of
P pull who could live together with no
Q pid to commence their love for each other!
R you able to see that this is the only way?
S pecially the way things are today.
T ch Man to respect Man and
U will see a great Earth de
V ate from what exists now.

W er love and triple your kindness and
    what you may
X pect is peace for all, but wonder
Y it took so long for Man to finally
Z.

THE BE OF BEING

I, for the sake of I, shall, for that very reason, I.
Shall should have I had been for me for short
a way not known?
No.
Why?
Just no.
Too brief a depth of want. Too fast a lonely cry.
Let me say, to make my point. Point. Point.
Could I have been as though it was to be for me
a being?
No.
Why?
Just no.
But, be is not the not of nothing. It every part
Of is is is, is it not?
No.
Why?
Just no.
But, getting closer to be is being. That **is** is! Is it
not that not is is? Right to say of saying is
not is is. Therefore, is is is also is not. But, is not
is not is not? For, saying as we do already, it **is** so.
So?
No.
Why?
Just no.
Wait!

So be is being not the not of nothing, not just being be.
Good! That's it! Why?
No.
Why no?
Just no!
Oh, I see!

RED CARNATIONS

It is windy down by the water's edge
And they say it is very cold this time of year
But I don't feel the cold you know
And I barely feel the wind as I rest within my thoughts
Of her
I watch my fingers create a magical beauty
As they travel through her soft, sleek hair
Each silky thread seeks a place to hide
While all the scurrying rays caught up inside
The silky softness whisper "Ah, Ah, Sleep"
I can feel the powers of silence now
As the tugboats chase each tiny ripple
Made by the same strong wind
I don't feel the strong wind anymore
It's just as though I see myself
In the background of my mind
We have been here, For days, it seems
Watching each other's life pass
Watching our love…grow
And seeing how easy it is to live
I feel her press my hand around her waist
As we talk of stars, and love,
And us
Imagine:

The type of girl I have grown to love
She' s what every man dreams about, but more
She's all that I have ever hoped to find
And yet, I love her more than
Well, what **is** there except her?
She is my happiness, my Paradise
She is all the things I will ever want
Rolled up into a tiny package
Of soft, loving Love
Oh! She's such a very precious one
And I don't think about loving her
Even about how we came to be so close
I don't have to
The love I have for her is not the type you hope for
It just comes to those who wait
As the tide comes in and wets our feet
We know we must go
But we'll be back, very soon, and not in dreams
Then, as I touch my lips to hers
And whisper we must leave
She says she's always wanted a cattail
We get up from the sand
And walk along the beach
I tell her I will get her a cattail
Or red carnations

REFLECTIONS

There they are again my love
The water's quiet now above
There's one, there're two!
What's that? I see you!
In all this time, have we but seen
Ourselves beneath us? Has it been
Our own two bodies lying there
As still as is the water where
Those crystalline reflections wear
The image of a perfect pair?

He moves to whisper in her ear
And as he does he draws her near
They cuddle close midst mossy slopes
Exchanging dreams and highest hopes
The moon's full face is now revealed
Their true love's vow so tightly sealed
Neither Time, nor pain, shall e'er again
Destroy their passions firmly lain
Among the reeds and peaceful rills
And on the slopes of wheat-strewn hills

In twilight tranquil, upon stars I gaze
You, beside me, rest all the while I daze
And think of you, midst hues of blue
As soft as petals sweet sewn with dew
On water's edge we swiftly dance

In keeping with our lover's trance
All this I see beneath us there:
Our own two bodies lying where
Those crystalline reflections wear
The image of a perfect pair

SOME DAY MY LOVE

Sitting, dreaming, halfway glancing
My mind's eyes are still romancing
Thin lines of light by lash divide
Your lovely face my thoughts provide
Last night we met and now I'm free
The love I've searched I can now see
Reclining, sweet visions of love
I surely see, but, cannot touch
For, they are you and you are far away
Some day, my love. Some day. Some day.
Your voice, I hear not as a sound
A song that makes my heart resound
With joy I drift midst thoughts of you
All things seem sweet with morning dew
These things I pray when darkness rips:
To touch with mine your virgin lips
Dreaming, soft golden thoughts
I surely see, but cannot touch
For, they are you and you are far away
Some day, my love. Some day. Some day.
That night, alone, in our own way
Our eyes begged the other to stay
In staying one moment longer
I felt warmer, greater, stronger
I floated high that night, with you
The future holds so much to do
Remembering, wonderful moments

I surely see, but cannot touch
For, they are you and you are far away
Some day, my love. Some day. Some day.
To be without love is pointless
But, without **you** love is darkness
My passions run full course for you
Your love alone my prayers pursue
A princess from Heaven I've found
For you alone my heartstrings pound
Wishing, a blissful life
I surely see, but cannot touch
That life with you
Some day, my love. Some day. Some way.

I PASSED THE DAY WITH THE SUN

I saw the sun's first rays
Tiptoe over the trees at dawn of this day
And now it is already time for them to go.
I watched them all day. They had many moods.
Some were good, some bad, but each was very splendid.
Yes, even when rays bounced from pieces of metal or glass
In the sand by the roadside
Or, came shooting down at various angles
And seemed to denote a mood of anger or discontent
As they cut sharply through leaves
And made fish swim deeper under water
When they came down full force
On the back of the farmer's neck
Each of these things telling me
The sun was furious about something
Even then, there was a beauty, a goodness
It's kind of like the beautiful Irish lady
With her splendid temper
She will get magnificently angry
Over something small, turn red in the face
Stomp her feet furiously
But, never once lose her grace or elegance
When we were getting up
I think I was in a less agreeable mood than the sun
I had had a hard night, restless, I mean
For, sleep had not been easy. Thinking came easier
As I lay awake for several hours

While my mind was flashing hues and shapes at me
In an array, oft times I could not distinguish
I know why I did not sleep, why I would be bothered
But not why my mind would need so much time
To find out what, it seems now
Is so simple an answer

So, with a heavy head I rose
And waited for my friend to come
Over the plane of poplars
Gracing the edge of the meadow
Where I used to run my horses
As I waited, half-reclining on the grassy slope
By the south end of the garden
I could hear the pre-dawn animals
Making their characteristic noises
Each significant of its place in Nature's world
Some were going to bed after an active night of gathering
Worms, or bugs, or nuts, and some were just rising
Like the Mockingbird that is still singing
In the giant elm above me
We have been talking for a long while
He's a beautiful bird, all fluffed up with pride
And he has a beautiful voice
I try to imitate some of his calls
To see if he feels they are good enough
To deserve a reply

Sometimes, because he's a good-natured friend
He answers even my worst calls
It was good to pass these hours with him
When the sun reached the plane above the trees
I could see his face
He smiled and told me it would be a brighter day
That is how the day passed for me
Sitting under this elm, on the grassy slope
By the south end of the garden
Through my own many moods the sun kept me company
Except for short spells of cloudiness
Always smiling and telling me it would be a brighter day
But, it wasn't as simple as that
For, my thoughts won over and were my master
Even with the sun, and birds, and beautiful wind
To keep me company
I was lonely

MANBREAK

Entire oceans dissolved in air

Such tumult! My strength could not bear

Seas parted, as clouds touched the earth

Resounding, splashes crashing, birth

To a new queen I now succumb

Another man I am become

BLIND MAN'S HOLIDAY

Hot breath in my face
Salt spray is my tea
The sun is standing
On top of the sea
Waiting for darkness
To blanket my ship
Fast, long, golden lines
Do silently slip
From one point straight at me
Then, like magic, around me
Somehow, they all miss me
And start, then, behind me
To go on forever
And with them goes brightness
With only my image
Distorted in darkness

I WISH FOR YOU

I wish for you this special day
That all good things shall come your way!
As you get up and don your clothes
Honor this day with pretty bows
Two bows of ribbon in your hair
One for color and one for flair
This day is yours, 't is made for you
It starts right now with morning dew
A sundry of hosts, all, in one night
Prepared in haste upon this site
All kinds of treats, wondrous things
Each made for you from Nature's springs
Each thing is done and in its place
This day they especially grace
For you, the sloping moss is lain
And little brooks full-brimmed with rain
Forest flowers are in full bloom
Each one a bride, each one a groom
Gay birds are fluffed and full with song
Sweet notes for you last all day long
A gentle breeze, as clouds skip by
Through trees, which bend on high
You'll see these things today and hence
As Beauty, Grace, and Innocence
That all these things shall come your way
I wish for you, this special day!

THIS HAPPY SOUL

Sweetly guide my little wooden ship
To lands unknown and free
Where drunken elves and fairies trip
And play beside the sea
Run swift! Oh, great, blue tide
Run swiftly, freely free
This happy soul, with pride
I now commend to thee!

ODE TO LOVING

It is Love that makes life's light orb
cast Hell's shadows to Hell in the morning.
For me, anyway. And I know, truly, when I
love her most, because my mind frolics
through bejeweled fields and sunny ways.
But, as my whole novel of emotions writhes
in gross sighs I feel as though the sky's
umbrella will never lift from my window sill.
Thank God it always does, so that my entire
soul's passionate yearning for her feels
stronger and I can make it through the
darkness once again.

It is Love that makes whole mountains take
wing and fly from the foamy froth of a fiery
sea. For me, anyway. It's just one very
wonderful feeling I hold for life. And what
sweet rhapsody it is! The massive armies of the
world with all their marching, together, cannot
within an hundred millennia trample a single
amaranth, while my love joyfully jostles great
galaxies with no more than a pinky. Although
we are apart sometimes, because I know it
must be, the diary of all Time, a beautiful
white pyramid forms so swiftly we seem
to be together again before we even bid adieu.

All the while my drooling tongue feasts upon
rabid thoughts, my mind's mouth's loins lip
her own and I feel as much a part of life
(and Love) as dapples to a fleeting fawn,
beauty to a masterpiece drawn; like
stars to a starry night or wings to a bird in flight.
It is Love that enables Love to employ
entire empires of intense emotions to
inflame the effervescent youth in every
heart of a million me's ten trillion times
with a single glance. For me, anyway.
And to soothe my rough palms on her
wintered silk tapestries is like no
paradise ever expressed with written words
by man. Loving her is loving life and living
with her is like living a life of Love. I'll wager
Love is that beautiful unseen Authority who
persuades each faithful retainer in Nature's
lusty arena to shake off Night's Stygian
essence, sponge up the morning's crisp shower
and go forth from fantasy's favorite fountain,
as a falcon flies from its fancier. And I'll bet
she's the same wonder who will gently quiet
the day's inquietude, harness the
unharnessable, stop that which she had
started, soften all of the day's hardness,
put peace to all and sleep with each.

Then she, alone, shall keep vigilance
against Bane's veil until the break
of dawning next.
It is Love that makes the perpetual pendulum
penetrate, suddenly stop, stand still so strangely
as each voluptuous volume vibrates and every
second is a delectable eternity. For me, anyway.
And, sometimes I do not see her, but I can sense
her presence through every pore as though
she is all around me and I cannot help
being her. When she speaks to me (Oh! How
she speaks to me!) it seems like I'm listening
to my heart throb, my very own breath of life.
I cannot help loving her, for, she **is** Love.
For me, anyway.

OF FRIENDS AND LOVERS

It's not such a secret place

Your land of tears

I've strolled its winding walks

Forlorned for many years

Please, do not heave and each place go

With heavy sighs

Don't look ahead at life

Through salt-stained and blind eyes

Think not of dark clouds only

Live in dreams and we

Shall find a peace together

From shadows we'll flee

No, it's not such a secret place

Your land of tears

Have faith in life with love

And ended are all fears

A MOUNTAIN FROM A CLOD

Four candles each are lit and all aflame
To write by their light is my one clear aim
Just now, I sit at this oak-leafed table
The cold winds push my thoughts and I'm able
To feel, but **taste** each part of Life and Death
That eats, imbibes my brain, as each quick breath
Drops to the chasm of my inspired chest
My whole self sweats and heaves in this fierce test
A wolf's howl cuts through my shirt and rips out flesh;
Shreds of my back fall as I scream, doubt
I can go on, but must, for, if I fail
To get down now, these thoughts, just as the hail
They'll melt, while winds watch the sun coming out
My thoughts, unlike most plants, don't grow by sprout
Not true-felt thoughts, emotions, creations
Surely, for these are such derivations
That cannot be but from a nobler source
As from our God or some similar force
I say the wind, the rain, the coldest cold
And other strengths of mighty Nature mold
Our greatest thoughts while we are not aware
But into space or rolling oceans stare
I say 't is death and war, with all their pain
Among the rest that so stirs a man's brain
Into confusion first, but then to sense
As the Poet is born, and, in his tense

Dark mood builds whole mountains with words; his verse
Is made, so smooth in form, but, rough in thought
Each age our greatest scholars have fought
And tried to untangle those lofty lines
Composed in words only, but, aged like wines
So that their savor is increased, from sweets
To rich nectars of past gods. Each one treats
That diligent student of Truth the past
Hopes and dreams of men, who, in that long, vast
Void of Time set down their hearts' own song
As I tonight will try to do with help from God
Or Nature's will in wild unrest, though, at my nod
Shall leave me, to create a mountain from a clod
Mine, later, to be picked apart and then downtrod

MAGIC ACT

One silver thread of frozen breath just falls

To crash below upon the leaves, where soil

Is rich and black. One caterpillar crawls

In magic glee to spread his silken coil

Around him once, again; each time he goes

A little more himself within does close

To sleepy state he soon befalls, and takes

His leave, this world to wait his dawning day

Time's glass has filled and let 'til yon day breaks

And silken threads grown hard have split and lay

Aside, a little slit to stride, one head

In newborn shape appears, and soon, by shakes

And twists its cozy mid-life's bed is shed

Thus, freed from Earth, one common servant wakes

DAFFODIL

A silly notion
(Thank Heaven for silly notions!)
Ushered me from my bed
And into pre-dawn wanderings
In search of you
My feet and legs so soaked
With dew from leaves and grass
Scratched by greedy branches and thorns
Through which I tramped
With half-shut eyes
Carried the weight of my desire
Until the sun came through the trees
(Though not at once)
To show me where
you hid

RUBY RED
(or, **SONNET TO THE RUBY RED**)

I had told them I would do it
But this I can remember well:
My ruby red in vein was writ
Was seeping, creeping through each cell
I told them: soon they would grieve me
But, O! They did not believe me
And, so, I let my ruby red
Run free upon the bedroom floor
It ruby-shot me in the head
And rubied too, my clean, white door
And both my legs were rubied too
My brain did twirl and to my bed
I seeping, weeping flew
And there did I drop dead

WHOREWITCH

I

Filth goddess, wanton slut
Portrait of the mind's low lust
Descend these murky depths, lay
Roll within the thoughts vile waste
Bile so rank and grossly based
Its stench is lost to slobs
Trapped within your dark domain
Each moment they breathe, they die
Slipping, sliding, creeping shit
Your oozing muck silent slips

II

Evil stagnate, World's Whorewitch
Perverse gore and ill-thought rot
Huge waves of mudcrust sludge fall
Crash, then break, lie unbroken
Pages printed, colored in
Filled with scenes of course, foul crap
Your authors' minds uncreate
And destroy much noble thought
To find your cave, seek you out
Always there, they pull you out
Put you in to show the world
Its tragic death in blindness

III

Hellqueen! Life's hopes dank darkness
Your death, my quest; they're the same
To see your dark, dry bones split
And be cast out from the earth
In space to be shot, direct
To strike the sun; war in fire
The battle's short: you are lost
Perished in a separate Hell
Making death a Hell in Hell
The awful, ugly death, you

GOD'S HONEY

My silly looks of awe and amazement
Are all used up so quickly here
Where the whole world breathes itself upon me
If ever Love and Beauty were Music
So truly I feel each happy tree's bending rhythm
In rhapsodic felicity at this moment
I cannot point
To a single Whippoorwill singing
Or one leafy Birch's gentle whisper
To one innocent Monarch's love for one
Satiny petal on this bountiful creek bank
That tiny Fawn I saw but seconds in splendor
One moment's peace with a friendly wind
A single hour's graceful symphony of sweet songs
The flood of my whole world's happiness
Cannot be described within the puny bounds
Of a mortal's words
I dare not show you any one
Of these dearest things
Which permeate the world around me
For, they are all in one
The Beauty and Magnificence
That enthralls my soul in wonder
As my mind drinks these sweetest nectars
I cannot point to any one
While my eager hands are outstretched
Enveloping whole acres
Of God's Golden Honey
The Rainbow Castle of my Dreams

ON ANGELS' WINGS

My hand and arm were cramped as knots
And all sense long since gone
Still, my furious pen spilled forth
Its swift, sweet blood upon
Whatever it could kiss. I could not
Dared not stop my pen
Its course was lain and ran
Beyond the course of mortal men
My fev'rish, sweating frame grew limp
And seemed as if to die
Then, suddenly, it quaked a bit
And soon began to fly
Beyond the clouds and into space
A part of me did wing
For, far behind, my mind gave up
For, with it, 't could not cling
My speeding, streaking brain did make
A bold attempt to catch
Each streaking, speeding thought
But, obvious to me, the match
Was brain against an unknown force
My mind against all minds
With such awe I cowered low
To 'wait this greatest of finds
However hard I'd tried, with faith
I could not, did not win

That my own hand, and arm, and pen
My very mind, I swear
Did part in substance and in deed
And pass into the air
So, to, did all that e'er was real
Upon this earthly sphere
Quick-split and fade away
And into darkness disappear
But, at the instant of the moment
That all began to fade
I perceived and loved the Force
Of which I'd been so afraid
Oft times in mysterious forms
Our deeper spirits see
What moves and grows inside each thing
And brings Eternity
How can it be that we foresee
In dismal, dreary gloom
Ourselves enchained in fiery deaths
Within an endless doom?
I cannot help but see such folly
Just now, as I look back
And realize how easily
Had I turned white to black
I had not been with reason kept
As I had liked to think

But, to a wanton blindness had
My soul been pleased to sink
But, now, in peace and harmony
Do all the pieces fit
For I have learned that I, Poet
With other Poets sit
To contemplate and glorify
And so to use our wit
That we may show the sleeping world
What words our God has writ

AGAIN, THE HAPPY EXILE

Do not think that hidden orb of day's daylight
Has passed its course e'en once
Since last I gazed and was entranced
Within your eyes, so fire-tossed
And full of fury
That your soft lines upon my dreaming
Have been a clear and present calm
Not thirty times have silent grains
Come falling down
And raised their graceful pyramid
Within an hour's glass
That in my thoughts, within your arms
Have I yet failed to be
And played as thunder god on fluffs of clouds
In moments of sweet repose
The frozen face of our own Venus
Goddess of the night and Love
Has not been seen upon my sill
Or wandered through far bogs of Time
For more than one short moment's span
While, through my throbbing chest in tight embrace
Your splendid frame in hopes was held
Fear not that morning dew's sweet morning kiss
Has graced the lillies lips and played
Its rainbow game

On waking rooster's restless wails
But once since all my hopes were born
And in these moments fleet of foot
Your fair tresses graceful touch
Has to my face been known
't is true, fear not
Each waking instant's sweet caress
Within my mind's domain
Has been my friend, and such a treat
To simple joys I've nurtured from within
While building altars all aflame for you

ON MAN'S ETERNAL BATTLE

Weary soldiers in the fields
Broken helmets, swords and shields
Children weeping for their bread
Families sorting through their dead
Missiles streaking from great guns
Striking someone's country's sons
Bullets, bombs and other tools
Made by men make bloody pools
Some men live to show their wives
Arms and legs hacked off by knives
Bloodied from their fierce blood feast
Victims of the great War Beast
Millions fight, but don't know why
No one learns, except to cry
Countless miles of virgin soils
To **no** victor go these spoils
Protests made are swept aside
Nothing's heard where kings reside
In the endless search for peace
Man renews his next war's lease

Published in:
The Plowman, Ontario, Canada, 1990
Whispers In The Wind, National Library
Of Poetry, 1993

THE BERRY BUSH

The Tree of Life was bending low
As clouds on high blew swiftly by
Sweet newborn leaves did kiss the snow
And sheltered fields from Winter's sky

As icy roots began to thaw
The sleeping Ides of March awoke
Spring's busy moths began to gnaw
And tear away last season's cloak

At base of giant, bending tree
A berry bush was nearby found
For months I watched, but could not see
A single seed upon the ground

But, as the cruel and bitter frost
Gave way to warmer, brighter days
Such pretty birds returned and tossed
The barren branches in strange ways

It wasn't long, then, as I watched
For, soon one tiny bud did sprout
And clumps and beads of blossoms notched
Each branch and berries soon popped out

This tiny bush bore golden crop
And left its trace for me to see
The seeds now chewed from beaks did drop
As little birds fed full with glee!.

THE FLAME

I do not question of our love
Its origin or strength
But turn, instead, to Him above
To thank and praise at length
In gratitude for Paradise
Wherein I'm blessed to be
I pay what seems so fair a price
And live on a bent knee
I do not know of many men
Who on this sphere find bliss
But, I, as Mary Magdelene
Have felt His gracious kiss
And though the Scripture says He is
An angry, jealous God
I am a faithful son of His
Who, by His Love is awed
He gives me you, to love and keep
To cherish in this life
And so, on earth, on you I heap
The honors due my wife
As long as I do not forget
Whence came this lovely peace
God's jealousy will be offset
His love for me'll increase
The day I love you more that He
(Though love you less I can't)

His gift of you will part from me
An excommunicant
I'm not fearful, but devoted
I can surely love you both
Thus I swear, as I denoted
And take the Holy Oath

Published in:
The Plowman, Ontario, Canada, 1991

MY LADY LOVE

In flow'ry bed, 'midst nuts and fruits

My lovely lady lay

Her sunlit hair, from tips to roots

A rainbow display

A gentle breeze did kiss the air

And colors danced about

Sweet fragrant scents flew here, flew there

't was heavenly throughout

To lazy state did I become

A spirit in the sky

But once did I approach this queen

And kiss from up above

My heart leaped up for I had seen

The face and shape of Love

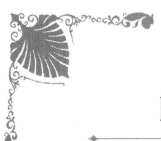

DESERT SONG

Ah! Such surprise!
The rain that fell
Upon this dusty desert town
All early misty morning yesterday
So clear, so soft
So beautiful today
To wet the sand
The whispered moisture
From the pre-dawn sky
Upon such tranquil shades
Of rusty mountains
Standing out of the ground
Making horizons closer
Bluer
Grayer
All shades of brown
And red
Making song jump up
Amidst tall cactus statuettes
Sun-tempered palo verde
Ah! The laughing willow!
Not weeping here
All the life here's laughing
Dancing with the autumn breeze
Singing with the rain
Ah!
All the quiet noise!

FLOWER SONG

I

O! Sweetest flower that I know
Let's watch the daylight come and go
The sun comes up, the sun goes down
Your lovely face 'neath dew drop crown
Your arms, when all at once you wake
Such tiny, silent circles make
A waterfall of bending light
Is formed, as waning trace of Night
Begins to faster, faster flow
And races for the soil below
Through blades and leaves
The morning breeze
In happy song brings sleepy bees
Each tiny friend with eager tongue
Licks dew drops till your spirit's flung
Into the clouds and far beyond
And, thus, a sparkling new day's dawned

II

This preparation now complete
You're anxious to the new day meet
You spread your snowy, silken sleeves
While sunlight through your body weaves
A trace of light through each part bends
Such splendid hues great Nature blends

The sun now rises in the sky
To watch huge, puffy clouds roll by
The greatest portion of each day
You grow, and with the windy sway
Of trees and bushes all around
Each passerby with grace astound
A joyous day you bring to all
Until the sun begins to fall
As darkness settles o'er the field
To nighttime slumber you must yield

III

Upon the plane of Mother Earth
The sun, eyes closed, assumes her berth
The Golden Goddess of the Night
Gains spirit for her upward flight
And when this Queen and all her Stars
Have reached their summit, yon, like Mars
A daytime world is wooed to sleep
And gentle rest day's life forms reap
You too, my lovely, dainty friend
Must fold your arms and backward bend
Thus, sleepy state your vibrant frame
Will wear tonight and play its game
As silent rest paints on your face
A very special, Godly grace
Content for eons, we shall fly
My lovely Amaranth and I

SONG OF THE FAIRY

Sweet, childhood days one day my mind
Did wander to and woo
Those countless hours was I inclined
To dream of only you

The day was bright and full of life
A great elm overhead
Below, I whittled with my knife
And sometimes stories read

This day was, too, a special day
In some ways like the rest
But on this day a windy sway
Upset a lofty nest

A bunch of twigs on tiny limb
Was carefully designed
But, in the wind, tipped on its rim
And toward the ground bee-lined

From in my sleepy, daydream state
I heard a gentle crash
And when I looked, I saw a great
Big, silken, flowing sash

That lovely ribbon wound around
A tiny, broken egg
My eyes grew big, for, they had found
Within that egg a leg!

I further pulled that long, bright sash
And gently raised the egg
Which, from its fall, that sash had lashed
And saved that little leg
I placed that prize among the leaves
And watched it roll about
The leg was kicking at the breeze
By God! Would it get out?

It was a strong, but dainty limb
That wriggled and writhed so
So graceful, smooth, and very slim
From top to tiny toe

First, tiny bits of white did flake
And fall off from the shell
But, soon, a larger piece did break
And also downward fell

I could not slow my racing heart
For, it was **full** with glee
I watched each piece of that egg part
The creature would be free!

On hand and knee I watched that day
And in amazement put
My spirit into fancy's play
I saw a second foot!

Just then, with one great effort was
The egg upset at last
While, with a whirring and a buzz
A little bug whizzed past

It has been but one moments span
Since first I'd spied that nest
And now my fev'rish thinking ran
To how I'd greet my guest

Adorned in golden daisy loops
With ferns and buds galore
Her costume was of flow'ry groups
Such fragrant robes she wore!

She was a tiny, graceful thing
And stood among the leaves
Such pleasure did her visage bring
Her silken hair and sleeves

Now, let me tell you, I was pleased
To view that pretty thing
Who slowly to my heart had eased
Herself to gently sing

In harmony and breezy notes
That little fairy sang
My anxious frame to clouds did float
Sweet forest chimes she rang

The notes were soft, her words so fresh
They filled the air with joy
A thousand goose-bumps lined my flesh
I was that lovely's toy

My lashes closed, my blood was stirred
I wafted through a cloud
Her song I cherished when I heard
Its songstress was so proud

These words, so sweet, were whispered there
Its message is supreme
And ever since that day I share
This song and all its dream

"I am a tiny thing to see
And, not so much to hold
But, if you're patient, you shall be
In youthful pleasures rolled
Pray, close your eyes and let your blood
Drink up my sprightly rhyme
And as the treats of Nature flood
Drift off and float in Time

There is no limit to the Grace
Within this world of bliss
So, as your eyes meet Nature's face
Please wear a gentle kiss
Within that kiss mold all your trust
In simple things that live
There is, in Nature's realm, a lust
So be the **first** to give
For this, we little fairies wait
To raise you from the ground
And lift up to a lofty state
Where pleasures all abound"

Her song complete, she flew away
But, first, she came close by
Upon my lips, she pressed that day
A kiss, and one long sigh

I was not sad to see her go
My little fairy friend
For, I can live on what I know
And all good things must end

Soon to be published:
Quill Books, 1997

DIANE

O! Woe!
How the days have darkened!
Miserable. Bleak. Desolate.
The seconds have passed
Without you here

Such bright, sunny days!
Gorgeous, but fleeting
Never fully appreciated
But truly loved
While you were here

Alas! Yet, you are gone
Still away
The clouds will not pass
And it is still very dark
Please . . .
Bring back the sunshine
I miss you!

DONNA

You know
Without expecting it
Each tiny gesture of love I make
Each little thing I give to you
Each of these brings such great joy
In the giving
And yet,
You never fail to give them back
Grown more beautiful
So much more magnificent
Ten-hundred-thousandfold
Than when I first gave them!

A DAWN

Cloudless blue skies
Bright
Endless
Left behind by recent waves
Of stormy cries
Bring welcome relief
From darker days
When worries seemed huge
Held against bleak
Black walls of rain
Ah! Bluest, deepest blues
Sweet sunshine
Chase away the darkened moods
Uplift hearts
To new heights of joy

Ah! Melodious Mockingbird!
The Mourning Doves!
How the glistening dew drops
Catch and propel
The early morning light
Sweet, gentle breeze
Gently nudges me from my bed
As I wander to work wishing
No more than to behold your lovely face
Once again
Enraptured by the beauty
Of each fleeting glance!

OH YOU

Oh you . . .
After so many long years
Such time lost, groping
Far, far past hoping
Lost in my private, lonely world
Who could have guessed
We, two, would meet and love
And be so right for each other
Now, though it seems years
Since the day I first met you
Only twelve days have passed
Such fun days!
Fantastic time tightly packed
Grand embellishment of every passing moment
From picnics, parks and weekend camping trips
Movies, parties, the beach and bicycling
Dinners out with very good friends
The State Fair, and
Quite splendid nights at home

I live for each moment,
Each second I can be with you
For, all time is bliss
When I can hold and caress
And care for you
I revert to a clod when you are away
In your sweet, wondrous ways

You kindle fires in me and bring to life
All my hopes and dreams
Oh you . . .
My love
Burning its way from my heart
Seeks to envelop you in its warmth

PARADISE

No mistaking your looks
Breathtaking
Taking me in ecstasy
Far, far beyond fantasy
To a land I can feel
From pleasures I reel
Where dreams are made true
My thoughts, moments with you
Paradise
Bliss
Already in Heaven
I wax immortal

FOR YOU ALONE

For you alone, always, will I live
While hoping, with all the love I give
The caring, devotion you can see
The True Love
My heart of heart's set free
Such sweet seconds
Each moment's passing
Glorious memories amassing
Such bliss my once lonely spirit shows
As the purity of my love grows
And grows
And glows
For you alone, always, will I live

SUMMERWINTERTIME

Though verdant hills have long since browned
And frosty breath falls on the ground
My spirits fly, my hopes are high
With glee and joy I happy cry

Though bird and beast have southward flown
From cold that chills right through the bone
I bask and bathe in naked fun
As if I were a burning sun

Though icy winds assault the sky
And leafless branches downward sigh
No darkness visits this heart's home
Through sun-filled flow'ry fields I roam

Behold! The reason for my glee
The love, the hope you give to me
Such tenderness and caring ways
You've shown to me these Wint'ry days!

First published poem.
<u>World of Poetry Anthology</u>, World
Of Poetry, 1990
Winner: "Golden Poet," 1990 award
<u>The Plowman</u>, Ontario, Canada

BECAUSE OF YOU

How much I love my life, because of you,
    my wife . . .
If I put all of the nice things I feel for you
    in a box, I would need a box big enough
    to hold the earth!
Were I to take the time to write down all of
    the wonderful feelings I feel because
    of you, there would not be enough time
    in ten-thousand lifetimes, or pens, or
    paper enough to do so.
And, if I tried to hold you, and tell you all of
    the beautiful things you are to me, I
    would hold you forever, always, and I
    would not run out of things to say far
    into our next lifetime.
If you would let me, I would fill all of your
    time with me with loving tenderness . . .
    touching, kissing, caressing you, con-
    vincing you of my undying, ever-increas-
    ing love and devotion.
And, if I could yell loudly enough from the top
    of the highest mountain and tell all about
    the depth and strength and greatness of my
    love for you, my voice would break out from
    the bounds of this earth and fill the whole
    universe with shouts of joy, and happiness.

I cannot tell you how very much I love you, how much you give to me, how much I want to give to you; there are no words that can express these things, so, my Dearest, my Darling, if you will allow me to, I will gladly spend each sweet moment of my life with you, showing you in every way I can, how much I love my life, because of you, my wife.

YOU MEAN MORE TO ME

You mean more to me
Than words can ever say
Just to hold your hand
And to know our love will stay
Feels so right
When you're in my arms
My Love, tonight
Oh! You! You mean more to me
Than any love
I've ever known
And I want to give you all of my love
Just you alone
You are all of my dreams come true
There's so much joy in your eyes
And all of the love you give
You finally made me realize
You are all I need
Oh! You! You mean more to me
Than words can ever say!

A THOUSAND DAYS OF LOVE

As we begin our second thousand days together
I pause to reflect upon our first:
I've grown to know your many ways, and yet
Sometimes it's like we've only just met
Each day, you promise to be someone new
In every way a stranger, someone who
Is ever-exciting, full of mystery and life
Though three years ago you became my wife
The joy you bring me has no measure
Your love, your beauty, all, I treasure
The child-like wonder in your eyes
Unbridled dreams with hope-filled sighs
Your laughter, song, and tears
Your different moods throughout the years
The ways you only have touched my heart
You touched my soul right from the start
And, speak of touching! Ah! Your sweet caress
Makes me weak . . .your slave . . .helpless
My love for you (though great) keeps growing
In every way, each day glowing
My love for you I keep refining
A light, a fire, a beacon brightly shining

MORE THAN WORDS CAN SHOW

I've thought for hours how best to start
To tell you, Dear, what's in my heart
It's hard to start, but, when I do
I write the nicest things to you

The rush and noise, this frantic life
All of the trials, trouble and strife
Oft times I forget to tell you
Things go unsaid as if you knew

Now's a good time to pause and say
"I love you, Dear, much more each day."
And as years come, and, as they go
I love you more than words can show

HOW GREAT MY LOVE

These thoughts and feelings from my heart
I'll have for you, till death do us part
Such deep emotion grows and grows
No sweeter love a lover knows
To spend my life with you in bliss
And on your lips to press a kiss
I long to hold you close to me
And always love you tenderly
You are my stars, my sun, my moon
And that is why I sing this tune
Don't ever doubt how great my love
You are my hopes, my dreams, my dove

SO THANKFUL

When I am down, my spirits low
In Satan's grasp, to depths I go
The Evil One can work his ways
And plunders me for days and days

If I don't walk each day with God
Old Satan treats me like a clod
He tramples me, abuses me
No matter how I try to flee

In pain and torture will I live
Each moment I forget to give
My thanks to God, to bend a knee
And, praising Him, to be set free

In such a way, through fellowship
My loving God breaks Satan's grip
And no fears come while He's around
The angel's sing, sweet harps resound

Because I've learned to walk along
Each day with God, He makes me strong
Such strength that Satan cannot shake
My faith, nor evil progress make

No matter how hard Satan tries
To trick me, trip me with his lies
He stumbles flat upon his face
As long as I enjoy God's Grace

As I resist each urge to sin
Satan suffers, thus, I begin
Each day with praise to God above
So thankful I can know His love

ROZANNE

Reminisce
Love's first kiss
Kissing her, life's sweet bliss
Thus, my love grew and grew
Tender, caring, love so true

Sun's rays striking her hair
Bending, reflecting fair
Radiant, glistening
Lovely
Of thee I sing

Beauty fair, beauty fine
Fairest flower on the vine
Pure in mind, pure in heart
Piercing deep
Cupid's dart

She inspires
Kindles fires
Fueling all my hopes, desires
Thoughts of her, something more
O'er lover's clouds I soar

Still, my love grows and grows
Greater love no one knows
Love her always
Yes I will
Loving her, such a thrill

Through these lines I hope and pray
How deep my love, can I convey
How blessed I am to spend my life
With her, my love
My loving wife

OF THEE I SING

Beauty pure, beauty fine
Fairest flower on the vine
Pure in mind, pure in heart
Piercing deep
Cupid's dart

She inspires
Kindles fires
Fueling all my hopes, desires
Thoughts of her, something more
O'er lovers clouds I soar

Still, my love grows and grows
Greater love no one knows
Love her always
Yes, I will
Loving her, such a thrill

Through these lines I hope and pray
How deep my love, can I convey
How blessed I am to spend my life
With her, my love
My loving wife

LOVE KEEPS GROWING

There is no doubt within my mind
My love for her herein defined
I cannot hope to find one greater
There is no way to overrate her
I waited long, but, when I found
The love she gave made heartstrings pound
Eons passing while I waited
Till I met her I created
Visions of her without knowing
They'd come true and soon start showing
All the love so long I'd hoped for
She would give me freely, and more
Ever since that day we married
In such wedded bliss we've tarried
She's my sweetheart, dearest, lover
No one can be placed above her
I adore her; love keeps growing
Passions kindled, ever glowing

THERE IS NO LOVE THAT CAN COMPARE

There is no love that can compare
Our love is nurtured with such care
It grows and grows as time goes by
Such passions burning! My! Oh, my!

Our love is true, such devotion
We enjoy such deep emotion
As our love is based on giving
Giving makes our lives worth living

We are so blessed to live our life
Together, loving, man and wife
Our love growing, ever showing
Beacons in our hearts keep glowing

MY LOVE FOR YOU

Your silken tresses falling down
Beneath a gilded, studded crown
Your eyes like sunbeams, piercing, bright
I am entranced within their light
Your rosey cheeks so soft and pure
The fairest skin of all I'm sure
Your teeth so white between your lips
A cradle through which red tongue slips
Your neck and shoulders also make
A path to treasures and I take
Your loving arms around me tight
And hug you close with all my might
Your other features are as fine
I drink them up, a priceless wine
Your lovely, precious, through and through
And there's no love like mine for you!

Published in: <u>The Plowman</u>, Ontario, Canada
<u>Awaken to a Dream</u>, Watermark Press, 1991
"Sound Of Poetry" audio cassette, Watermark Press

THE ONLY THING I NEED

Though one more year is soon to close
My love for you still grows and grows
I pause to write in these spaces
How much my life your love graces
You cannot know how much it means
Such lovely, tranquil, pleasant scenes
Are in my dreams, sweet dreams of you
Because, my love, my love is true
So, as we close another year
I hope my feelings are made clear
The only thing I need in life I have:
You are my loving wife

AND DARK CLOUDS BLEW IN

I spend my days. . . and nights. . . alone
Such melancholy have I known
As time passes, yes, each new day
Brings sorrow while you are away
There is no peace...the tears I weep
Make rivers, black and cold and deep
And pains within my heart of hearts
Strike deep, slash through, cruel, piercing darts
So much torment must I endure
Without you with me I am sure
There is no peace, no pleasures sent
To grace my life, I am not meant
To have relief, my life's a Hell
I hurt so bad and want to yell
To scream, to cry, release the pains
Such misery upon me rains
Yet, no joy comes, my life's a ruin
Since you left and dark clouds blew in

Winner: Award of Merit, Great Free Poetry
Contest, 1990

Winner: Golden Poet-1991, World of Poetry
Published: <u>Selected works of our World's Favorite Poets,</u>
World of Poetry, 1991

LOVE BITES

How many words have I written
When, by Love's bug I was bitten
Each time my heart sent up its song
Each time for you my heart did long
Sweet passions stirred within my mind
Such loving thoughts of you defined
Within your arms I long to live
And no one else my love to give
You are the only one for me
You are the best, you set me free

RENDEZVOUS

A chance and fleeting rendezvous
Sweet moments…sweet moments with you
Separation…life without you
Purgatory…I never knew
Trust me…I will do anything
For, I love you…and thus I sing
Your praises, spent emotions cling
And to me greatest pleasures bring
You do not know the love you share
While I can stand beside you there
Imagine us…the perfect pair
In love…the greatest love we dare

DEEPEST PASSIONS DARE

My heartstrings pound
Such love I've found
Loving you
My heart's set free
I cannot help but bend a knee
In thanks to my great, sweet Lord
Love's presents sent
I look up toward
A cloud-puffed sky
The faithful mirror
My mind's eye
Your brilliant face I see
In radiant beauty be
All love to you I swear
And deepest passions dare
My heartstrings pound
Such love I've found
Loving you!

ALL MY LOVE

From our first day of wedded bliss
Our love had grown and lover's kiss
Has graced our lips throughout the years
To others, great our love appears

Each day with you is such a treat
You are the nicest, sweetest sweet
In every way you are the best
I love you more than all the rest

So great the pleasures that you bring
You make me feel like I'm a king
And when you hold me close to you
I feel so warm, our love's so true

So, lovingly, I'll hold you near
And always cherish you, my Dear
Upon you all my love I'll heap
My love for you so true and deep

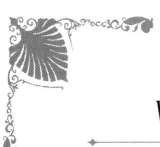

WITHOUT YOU

You cannot know the pain I feel
Each moment passing does reveal
The hell my life has now become
Such bitter pain that makes me numb
I thought I had things bad before
And did not know that less was more
I had it all and did not know
From little things great things grow
I cherished not the good within
Now take it hard upon the chin
These lessons learned are hard to bear
Such punishment! A shroud I wear!
I cannot stand the pain I'm in
Too long without you have I been!

FOREVERMORE

Chance meeting
Brief, fleeting
Two bodies pass
Lonely lad, lovely lass
Never knew before
Now know forevermore

Sweet moments shared
As two hearts bared
And souls did mingle
And heartstrings tingle
And love bells jingle
Chance meeting
Brief, fleeting
Two bodies passing
Loving memories amassing
Never knew before
No know forevermore

Touch. Touched. Touching.
Blissful feelings clutching
Lovers shared that day
But now are gone away
Chance meeting
Brief, fleeting
Two bodies passed

Loved once, but fast
Such love will ever last
Never knew before
Now know
Forevermore

HEART OF HEARTS

I waft through clouds at Heaven's door
And cannot hope to love you more
In loving you I'm made a king
As greatest treasures you do bring
You are my greatest dreams come true
I'll always have sweet dreams of you
And each time dreaming my mind starts
To smile at you, my heart of hearts
While, smiling back, you look so fair
My heart of hearts, our love so rare
Pray, can I tell you how I feel?
Just touching you makes me reel!

HOT FOR YOU

You may not know what you have done
But kindled flames as would the sun
And stirred the embers deep inside
That cooled with Time had nearly died
Brought back to life and blazing now
In such ways only you know how
Thus, blazing will they ever be
The flames your love has fanned in me

Published in: <u>In A Different Light</u>,
National Library of Poetry, 1992

THE CANDLE

Though I'm guilty of many crimes
And I have failed during hard times
I've hurt myself and others too
Can't believe I even hurt you
I was so proud, so vain, so lost
Never knowing what this would cost
The pain, the suffering each day
I did endure, in darkness stay
Through the misery I have learned
Despite my sins a candle burned
Until I finally saw its light
A far-off, warm, and pleasing sight
It took me long to see it there
Radiant, rising in the air
For many years I could not find
This candle burning, I was blind
I didn't know and tried to fight
Stayed far away from candle's light
Too bad! For all those many years
Were wasted with so many tears
Wasted because I could not see
You were calling, Lord. Calling me!

OUR SHINING ARMOR

As we pray here, humble, kneeling
More and more Scripture revealing
The Truth and Light, a mighty sword
We now raise up for our sweet Lord

As we surrender to His Word
Delving deeper, spirits stirred
Understanding His Word frees us
We now worship our sweet Jesus

With devotion and all our love
We place our faith in Him above
And for our faith our loving Lord
Will heap on us such great reward

We arm ourselves, prepare to fight
Our armor shining, shining bright
Assembled now upon the fields
Before our might all evil yields

And, thus, is mean old Satan bound
We trample him into the ground
And, slaying him with shining sword
A testimony to our Lord!

GLORY

Majestic eagle perched on high
Unfurls his wings, prepares to fly
To leave the nest, begin his quest
Will travel far above the crest
Of rocky mountains passed below
To lands where exotic ferns grow.

This eagle, soaring far and wide
Will not return till he has spied
A tender morsel on the ground
Or nice sized fish that swims around.
His eyes, so keen, look to and fro
Creatures scurry and hither go.

From 'tween high clouds he makes his choice
But one shrill cry he then does voice…
The only warning he will give;
A short time more his prey may live
For, now, he folds his mighty wings
And into steep dive eagle brings
His strength and skill and downward streaks
And dives between great mountain peaks.

The racing wind beside him blows
Past trees and lakes he swiftly goes.
As he approaches, by and by,
His racing prey escape will try.
But, talons sharp, are soon within
A fleshy back and thus begin
To tear and rend…it isn't long.
The grip of death so sure, so strong.

Though running beast a mighty fight
Does make (a bold attempt at flight)
Our mighty eagle's skill's supreme.
From prey warm blood begins to stream.
The kill is done and no more pain
Shall visit this beast on the plain.

And now, our great, proud victor roars
His winner's cry as up he soars.
Within his grasp his prey is held;
't was swiftly and with good cause felled.
Now, two great beasts ascend the sky
And back to lofty nest will fly
While, patiently, three others wait:
Two little ones, and hero's mate

On his return the eaglets swoon,
Their faithful father back so soon.
And, thus, with eager beaks the feast
Is made and soon, the little beast
Has been devoured, its purpose done,
As eagles thrive beneath the sun.

Published in <u>The Plowman</u>, Ontario, Canada

THE REST OF MY DAYS

I find myself upon my knees
My loving Father hears my pleas
I start and end each day like this
No chance to pray will I dare miss
For, years went by while I lived alone
Such lonely seeds my choice had sewn
Each time he asked, each chance he gave
I turned away, He could not save
This fool, I was not ready yet
On earthly things my mind was set
Thank God my God did not give up
His patience flows from bottomless cup
He cared for me enough to wait
Until, at last, I'd tempted Fate
But once too much and landed lost
Broken, beaten, my folly cost
Me everything: my home, my wife
My job; almost cost me my life!
The sad part is: it could have been
So easy if I could have seen
Much sooner how wonderful His Love
Raining down on me from above
That's why I now spend so much time
Kneeling, praying, and writing rhyme
Devoted, thankful, full of praise
I love my Lord and hands I raise
Loving Him the rest of my days

THE WALL

I walk the fringe with careful strides
From fearful heights my view provides
Within clear sight two sep'rate lives
Not seen before, this wall denies
A view of both from down below
And thus the scene where most must go

This wall: a thin but lofty one
Though built of air is deftly spun
Of stone and mortar most are built
But this, of fear and pain and guilt
You see, this wall is raised up high
Between two worlds: one rough, one shy

't is raised in such a careful way
That most of us are forced to stay
Within the one and never go
Beyond the wall so we could know
Such love, such beauty there resides
This wall, from all, this beauty hides

THE HUSBANDMAN

Blue skies darken, huge clouds amass
How swift warmer, kinder days pass!
Heavy laden, Winter winds come
Leave feet and hands and face so numb
Empty stomach and spirits low
Hope waning, negative thoughts grow
Upon this rock and dirt I lay
On such a cold, hard bed I stay
Though Nature's Winter fills the air
Still Summer season's clothes I wear
I'm not prepared, how could I know
Amid the frost these fruits would grow?
And, ugly, bitter, thorny plants
Are all Life's cruel, hard harvest grants
The seeds I've sewn are now full ripe
From eyes these icy tears I wipe
Thus, I lay here, shivering, cold
Before my time I have grown old
There's no way out; I made my bed
I'll stay here, frozen, till I'm dead

ALASKA CALLING

Crystalline lakes and rolling rills
Mountain ridge and ravine
Spruce and evergreen tall and wide
Crying wolf packs close at hand
Home of the great bald eagle
Land of the midnight sun
Sundry treats of Nature flood
Not many men call this their home
But, home it is
Home for us
Because we make it so
Home sweet home!

THE HALF MILLION

To foreign soil our men have gone
As battle lines were swiftly drawn
Young women, too, make up the ranks
Of those who fill the trucks and tanks

A half a million from our side
Assembled now; our hope and pride
These are our sons and daughters there
Who soon a bloody war must bear

Yet, each brave volunteer has made
The choice to serve, protect and aid
A friendly nation (and our own)
From greatest evil man has known

You see, a cruel and vicious beast
Has raised his head and rules the East
His ruthless armies rape the land
Against this onslaught our troops stand

He must be stopped and though the cost
Will be quite high as lives are lost
Our brave young sons and daughters go
To war, this beast to overthrow

THE BRAVE YOUNG VOLUNTEERS

From farms and shops and service stations
All walks of life and many nations
Young men and women volunteers
Form greatest army seen in years
Though they have trained they never thought
They'd need those skills, for, peace was bought
So long ago, in wars gone by
But, now, to foreign soil they fly
As these assemble on the sand
And there prepare to make their stand
Those left behind who can't be there
Will pray, and yellow ribbons wear
We love these brave young volunteers
Who go to war despite their fears
They've gone to stop the awful Beast
Who fuels the hatred in the East
This maniac, Saddam Hussein
Has made it clear: during his reign
There'll be no peace in all the land
And now has loosed a mighty band
He wages war in Allah's name
To kill, to torture, and to maim
He makes his own casualties soar
To justify his "Holy War"

To stop this madman is the task
Restore the peace is all we ask
So, now, with all our hopes and fears
We send our brave young volunteers
We know our troops will meet the test
They are so brave, the very best!
They'll bring to task this loathsome pest
So from this horror we may rest
And then the troops may homeward fly
To loving arms as mothers cry
And banners bright, and many cheers
For these, the brave young volunteers

THE FAMILY CALLED "HEART"

There once was a man named Sid
And also Billy the Kid
A friend was named Merle
Then Billy's little girl
The names go on and on
So, please, don't forget Don
And Richard was new
As this family grew and grew
A newt and a frog
And Remo the dog
Each one was a cog
In a wheel with no moss
Rolling wildly across
And with it rolled Ross
Now, Crystal was picky
She moaned, "You forgot Nicky!"
"No problem," I said
"His name's in my head"
For, nobody's first
And nobody's last
No best and no worst
No matter how fast
Or slow a name's listed
Each one plays their part
In this family called "Heart"

THRILL SEEKER

Some men climb great mountain peaks
Others jump into thin air from airplanes
Some cheat the Reaper, risking all
For glories found in racing cars or bikes
In many ways these bold men find
The means to make their spirits fly
To stir the soul and squeeze the most from life
Such thrills derived from drops of sweat
And blood as life's lusty fluids flow
These men, such deadly deeds do dare
Each one their pleasure's passions soar
Yet I, unlike these men, obtain
The same, unbridled thrills of life
In such an easy, painless way
I risk no sweat, no blood, nor death
To taste the same sweet ecstasy
To feel the same exhilarating joy
The thrills I feel at least as great
Achieved by just one act
A simple, beautiful thing I do
The simple act of loving you

MY BABY'S GONE AWAY

I'm so sad and I hurt so bad
And all my joy is gone
'Cause my baby's gone away
Only pain and tears remain
From this hurt that goes so deep
And deprives me of my sleep
It makes me want to die
For, there's no more will to live
All that's left to do is cry
'cause I'm so sad and I hurt so bad
And all the joy is gone
"Cause my baby's gone away
And only pain and tears remain

OH CHULITNA!

Of all the lands I've ever seen
And all the places I have been
Of all the mountains, rocky, high
And cliffs and peaks that touch the sky
Of all the virgin forests wide
And all the rivers I have spied
Of all the vivid, vibrant greens
And all the pleasing, tranquil scenes
Of every bird or mighty beast
That lives and thrives within the East
Of all the lakes, deep blue and clean
No bluer, cleaner, more serene
Of all the fresh, pure, unspoiled air
No other skies can quite compare
Of all the moonlight ever beamed
And every dream I ever dreamed
Chulitna River now is where
All things are greatest and, I swear
I've never seen a nicer place
Bestowed with all of God's good grace
And no more far-off lands I roam
I'm **glad** Alaska is my home!

SLOW DOWN!

Urgent call of Life
Cataclysmic rush of passing existence
Tumult of thought and feeling
Hustle and bustle
Hither and thither
Running men and women
Going everywhere
And nowhere
Such fast, furious "doing"
Accomplishes ulcers
Achieving "burn-out"
Going the wrong way so quickly
Racing backwards
Getting ever farther away

Stop!
Smell the flowers!
Feel the sunsets!
Absorb the sweet morning dew!
Live the wonder of the Northern Lights!
Slow down and relax!
Enjoy each precious second of your life
Don't hurry so unconsciously to nowhere
Set a comfortable pace
Proceed with felicity toward a real goal
Set your eyes on Nature
Your heart on God
And watch the beauty of Life unfold!

EMERALD SLEEVES

As Nature pays her yearly call
And all around the leaves now fall
Down through the canyons North Wind comes
With lightning and the thunder drums
All Summer leaves were vibrant greens
Such vivid, verdant, pleasant scenes
But swiftly change, are shades of red
Are plum and yellow now instead
They tumble down onto the ground
To crash, in heaps, without a sound
And soon each branch is stripped and bare
Not till next Spring these robes will wear
Thus, for a Winter we shall see
This lifeless face on every tree
Until the frost begins to thaw
And we may watch wide-eyed with awe
As buds and blossoms then will sprout
And new growth once again pops out
At first, small buttons dot the trees
Then, foliage sways within the breeze
As color hangs as emerald drapes
Upon the branches Nature's capes
And everywhere the eye can see
On every bush and every tree
Those newborn shapes, those lovely leaves
Nature's clothing, her emerald sleeves

Soon to be published:
Best New Poems, Poet's Guild, 1997
Sensations, Iliad Press, 1997
A Treasury of Verse, JMW Publishing, 1997
Treasure the Moment, Quill Books, June, 1997

MIRACLES

Miracles great

Miracles small

Miracles, one and all

You reveal yourself

In Glory

And in wonder

You are my Lord

My King

My Savior

My Hope

You are my everything

You bless me

Beyond my wildest dreams

Miracles great

Miracles small

Miracles, one and all!

TO WINTER

Winds chill, and snow begins to fall
The colors pale, as landscapes fade
Snow lines toward horizons crawl
And days grow shorter, I'm afraid

Those long, hot days of Summer past
Are gone; now darkness is the king
The sun, just risen, sets so fast
A few last leaves to branches cling

The smell of Winter's in the air
And log fires burning more and more
Big, padded mittens children wear
While, chopping wood's a frequent chore

The sleds and sleighs will soon be out
And skis and snowshoes dusted clean
On every hill will children shout
Upon the snow a happy scene

To Winter months we look ahead
Though freezing cold and bitter days
No better days to ride your sled
Or sit and watch your fire blaze!

Soon to be published:
Through The Looking Glass, National Library
Of Poetry, Autumn, 1977

GOD'S GRACE UNFURLED

I've written lines throughout the years
Of joy, and hope, as well as tears
Each time I've written, through each line
I've painted pictures, made words shine
Assembled letters on a page
Once formed, such thought they do engage
Sometimes labored, perspiration
A sign on pages, inspiration
Came not from the proper source
But, from some other, darker force
Powers moving meditations
Take so many variations
But, some are not by God desired
Instead, by evil thoughts inspired
We must be careful when we write
And do so always in the Light
And know which power we must use
And not the Poet's Gift abuse
For, we are gifted with the skills
To mold men's thoughts with our quills
So, if we're always close to Him
He'll guide our pen and noble hymn
Our words will write and show the world
Our simple words, God's Grace unfurled

TRIBUTE TO THE TOUGH (Alaskan)

Alas! The color now is gone
Dead leaves have fallen on the lawn
The trees are bare and all around
The mountain peaks with snow are crowned
As Autumn breeze begins to chill
And frost returns to every hill
The birds fly South where skies are warm
And flee from coming Winter storm
As daylight fades and color pales
Cold winds arrive in bitter gales
The Tourist gone, for good reason
He cannot stand your Winter Season
But, you will stay here in the cold
You are so hardy, brave, and bold
You're tough, and tried, and do not run
To Southern climes and chase the sun
You'll stay right here and shovel snow
And build your fires while cold winds blow
You'll drink hot tea and sometimes rum
Holding your mugs in hands gone numb
You like it here…for good reason
There's nothing like the Winter Season
Though snowdrifts almost touch the sky
And piles reach more that twelve feet high
You grab your shovels, dig right through
Shoveling snow's about all you do

I was not kidding when I wrote
With tea and rum you warm your throat
You're tough, and tried, and do not run
And have to be to have such fun
That's why you stay here in the cold
You're tough (or stupid) so it's told

THROUGH HIM

As with Life's questions you strain
Such turmoil boils within your brain
Your thoughts, a damned revolution
Such dilemma and confusion
Instead of knowing solutions
Your mind is full of delusions
Instead of happy, you are sad
You could be sane, but you are mad
While you remain preoccupied
With worldly thoughts you are denied
The peace that comes when thinking's pure
So, now, this curse you must endure

Too long in darkness have you stewed
It's time my friend, to change your mood
A simple course you now may take
And, taking this, the curse you'll break
Reach out to God and hold Him tight
Put Him first and stand in the Light
Call His Name and you will remain
Within His favor and He'll rain
His Godly grace down upon you
Your mind and body He'll renew
Then, no more darkness will you know
Through Him, your life in Light will glow

SEND UP YOUR SONG

Of all the thought that e'er was thought
Or any concept ever taught
Of every subject ever mused
Or any rhyme a poet used
Of each and every written verse
However rough, however terse
One subject is above the rest
And simplest verse by far the best
No spinning webs with lofty lines
In simple beauty His Word shines
Hold on to this: the Scriptures show
The Way, as all believers know
So, if you wish to write a rhyme
Take hold of something most sublime
Place your trust in our sweet Jesus
And set your thought in verse that pleases
Send up your song, exalt His Throne
And let your love for Him be known
In doing this, you'll find reward
Beyond your dreams; a mighty sword
Your words may be and you may fight
A winning battle for the Right
Thus, with the simple words you trace
You help to show the world God's face
Send up your song, exalt His throne
And let your love for Him be known

THE PHONICS SYSTEM

A list of all the letters had to be made
B for this task could be attempted
C what can be done as I
D cide what
E ch letter will depict by its sound.
F you have any trouble reading this and meaning
    does not con
G eal, read each letter just as it sounds.
H is the hardest, so, we'll skip it.
I m sure you're getting it by now.
J ze are hard to use (unless you're talking
    about birds).
K pable phraseology and verseology can
    create very
L oquent expressions and by these we may
M ulate lofty concepts by which we may be
N raptured.
O ver every other instinct
P pul must take their
Q and step forward when they
R called upon,
S pecially when called upon from Above to
T ch others how to lead
U seful, productive lives. Re
V ling Truth to others will
W er happiness in the end and
X istence will be profitable
Y l you continue to help others
Z what Life is all about.

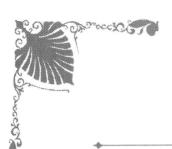

THE PEARL

That golden ball now creeping up
And warms me like my coffee cup
It pauses once, as if to pray
Though, only briefly will it stay
On mountaintop as darkness dies
And from its climbing Nighttime flies
As wee nocturnal creatures flee
The brightness shines on every tree
While rising up into the air
It passes through a thoroughfare
Of brilliant blues and clouds of white
And warmth comes with the pleasing light
For half a day this golden ball
Will rise and to its apex crawl
And, climbing up, bright rays will throw
That pleasing warmth on soil below
Then, when the upward climb is done
So soon becomes a setting sun
And, as warmth wanes the golden ball
Will to the West horizon fall
And, pausing once again to rest
Upon the far-off mountain crest
Its work now done, will slip behind
Until tomorrow when we find
It has returned and starts to rise
To once again warm Eastern skies

RAINDROPS FALL

We sit and watch as clouds sweep by
Another day of rain-filled sky
There are so many days like this
Sometimes the sunny ones we miss
But rain is good and as this squall
Relieves itself the droplets fall
And with their "pitter patter" sound
They pound like tom toms on the ground
As much as we enjoy the sun
We also love when rivers run
So, we won't mind when raindrops fall
We'll grab our boots and have a ball
We'll dance and tiptoe in the rain
To Nature's glory once again
We won't regret when rain clouds push
Their cargo down and muddy mush
Is everywhere as rivers rise
We come home soaked, 't is no surprise
So, we won't mind when raindrops fall
We'll grab our boots and have a ball!

TO THE WOODPILE

My firewood project now must stop
As snow piles higher on the top
Of all my logs, so, I will shirk
This task for now, I cannot work
Until this flurry has gone by
Then, again, the cutting I will try
The only problem is: it grows later
And depth to woodpile grows greater
But I'm inside my cozy cabin
And for a while at poem stabbin'
This is no meager, minor storm
As snowdrifts higher quickly form
It's blowing down onto the ground
And whiter getting all around
As snowflakes flutter all about
And kids with sleds begin to shout
And play, as snow piles higher still
It soon will reach my window sill
The paths I had cut through the snow
Now gone, they're buried deep below
A fresh new pile of Winter's white
As wood pile disappears from sight
I will not cut more wood today
In cozy cabin will I stay
And only hope that when snow stops

I can at least dig down to tops
Of woodpile project still undone
That, snow or not, I should not shun
When weather's good and there's no snow
To stop my chopping, don't you know

WINTER WONDER

't is true, for this we waited long
The Summer sun was burning strong;
It was so hot, so big and bright.
We waited for that scalding light
To wane, and for the milder days
To come, and as this year's Winter phase
Begins again to cool the lands
And frost upon the tundra stands.
As days grow short, a cooler sun
Now rises…Winter's thus begun.
Hints of Summer she erases
And on the ground snowflakes places.
She blankets all in virgin white
On landscapes paints a pleasing sight
As cold winds chase the azure sky
Now full of ice as crystals fly.
Each one a diamond, sparkling gem
A rainbow inside each of them.
And now you know why we waited
These Winter months anticipated:
Below, though all the life has browned
Above, with brilliant diamonds crowned
As over Mother Nature's face
This Winter Wonder leaves its trace

GOD BLESS MA BELL!

Blood still stirred
Breathing
Hard
Thoughts wildly wandering
Dancing
Goose bumps
Smiling similies
"Voice like sugar"
Sweet
Ringing
In my heart
Echoing enchantment
Lifting my memory
In ecstasy
Of all of you!

BESIDE MYSELF

I am beside myself with joy
You have made me a little boy
Knowing nothing, full of questions
Eager for your every suggestion
Without touching, you have touched me
Reach deep inside and set me free
Such wondrous miracles you make
As passions in me now awake
They make me want you even more
All things about you I adore
I yearn to hold you close, caress
Cherish you and gently to press
My warmth and love and lips on you
In every way, in all I do
To show my love and let you feel
The love I have for you so real
I am yours, all, so full of joy
A very happy little boy

TO THE ALASKAN MOTORIST

The snow came and without warning
Covers everything this morning
I would think this should not matter
Surely not this whole Earth shatter
But, I am shocked at what I see
What I'm seeing just cannot be!
You people live here all year round
And yet, you have not smart ways found
To get to work on days like these
When snow is blown by Winter's breeze
First thing of all, alarm clocks stop
When power fails as wires pop
Beneath the weight of snowy branch
That crashes like an avalanche
And so, you get up late to find
The engine of your car won't grind
For it's a frozen block of ice
And sitting there is not so nice
It finally starts and as it warms
More ice upon the windshield forms
Then, while the car is warming up
You go and grab your coffee cup
You will be late, there is no doubt
So you won't wildly run about
Each thing is planned so far ahead

And now...the shovel...in the shed
An hour later you have found
But now, snow's deeper on the ground!
Another hour and you're done
A path is cleared, the car has run
But brand new snow tires you had bought
Are in your trunk and you are caught

Without them now as you take heed
Of things you didn't think you'd need
So many others did not switch
To snow tires, so, within the ditch
The melee grows, as people shout
And beg the tow truck drivers to get them out
Then, not only is your wallet thinner
You feel just like a driving beginner
For, you cannot control your cars
And drive like people leaving bars
Into the ditch along the way
Another hour you will stay
Until a driver with a truck
Can manage to get you unstuck
And when that driver's done his part
You once again your autos start
To slip and slide on down the road
As if you thought it never snowed
Careening down the icy street

You soon, again, a ditch do meet
It's so late now, you might as well
Turn around; why go through the Hell
Of driving all that icy way
And clocking in at end of day?
You have now missed lunch, anyway
Which is no loss: you could not pay
(You know they don't take credit cards)
That's all that's left, as crossing guards
Usher children toward their homes
As, still, the morning melee roams
You just won't learn, as down the road
You go, as though it never snowed!

HEART AND SOUL

Can it be, these feelings felt
Make me weak, make my heart melt?
Just to hear your voice, so sweet
Within my ear a song complete
Melodious, soothing, refined
Magnificent portrait in my mind
And, longing, burning for your touch
Impatient, wanting you so much
You are the other half of me
Without you, there cannot be a "we"
I long to be again with you
And share the passions that we do
When we're together I am whole
Come home soon, my heart and soul!

FOR YOU . . .

Such things I yearn to do for you
Give you pleasures you never knew
It's hard to sit and dream like this
Throbbing, thinking of that kiss
I'll press, soft, upon your lips
With every touch your passion drips
Ebbs and flows each and every time
Into my loving arms you climb
I long to hold you in these ways
And lay with you for all my days
Caressing you I'll lift you high
Your quivering voice cries **"My! Oh My!"**
Such things, and more, I'll gladly do
All these I yearn to do for you!

THESE DREAMS OF YOU

Alas!
   There's nothing
Left to do
   But sit
And dream
   These dreams
Of
   You

Across these many
   Many miles
I feel
   You
Warmth
   Upon me
Smiles
   Such lovely visions
In my mind
   No greater pleasures
Will I find
   Than traces of sweet moments
Spent
   Within your arms
Before you went
   So far away
I now must stay
   Alone

~ The memories
~ The lovely you
~ I see
~ 't is all I have
~ 't will have to do
~ Till your return
~ And then
~ We
~ Two
~ May be
~ As one
~ Such bliss
~ Will share
~ Our lovers' hearts
~ Again
~ Lay bare
~
~ Then
~ I may give
~ My love
~ To you
~ And pleasures
~ Once again
~ Renew
~ Together
~
~ Together

Alone	~ Greatest joys
But, with you	~ We share
And I lay	~ Souls
Beside you	~ Touching
My dreams	~ Clutching
My only hope	~ Such love
My only hope	~ We dare!

    Until you can come back to me

SURELY YOU KNOW ...

Surely you can tell what you have done to me
You have heard my laughter
You have seen the bright twinkle in my eyes
You know you have never caught me when I wasn't
Wearing a big, exuberant smile
That could light up a room
You have seen me in my uninhibited joyfulness
As though I had reverted to a playful
Innocent child, oblivious to Life's hard rules
And disciplines, knowing only Life's simple
Minute-by-minute happinesses and freedoms
You can see the totality of my optimism
And hope, and faith, and confidence
You have listened to the quickening beating
Of my heart, the quickness being reciprocal
To how close I can be to you
Caused by the pleasure of your sweet presence
You also have heard my breathing grow
From slow deep breaths
To fast heavy breathlessness
As the thrill of you enraptured me
You have felt me shiver, from head to toe
Uncontrollable in the ecstasy of your embrace
You have felt my tender touch
The gentleness that you bring out of me
You have watched my eyes close

As I was made jelly, weak in your arms
As our mouths became joined
In such passionate, eternal kisses
You have read my poems and I have read some to you
And you have heard me tell you
In many other ways of the depth, sincerity,
Purity and greatness of my love and devotion
You have felt the secure feeling of trust
That comes by your knowing I am totally,
Completely, devoted and faithful to you alone
You have tasted my tears
As they rolled down my cheeks, and,
Knowing my sensitivity as you do
And that we've never had to share a sad moment
You know these must be my tears of joy
Demonstrating to you in what deep, beautiful
Ways you touch my soul and spirit
Surely you can tell what you have done to me
Surely you must know how very, very much
I love you!

SO DIVINE

I cannot tell you how I feel
By knowing you are really real
You are my greatest dreams come true
And I'm in Heaven loving you
I sometimes wonder if you are
The wish I wished upon that star
The way you came into my world
Just when my wishes upward swirled
And now you give such great relief
Erasing all my pain and grief
And make me feel like I'm a king
So many pleasures you do bring
You are so special and I know
Our love is true and e'er will grow
As lovely blossom on the vine
Eternal, blooming so divine

THE OTHER PART OF ME

I'd walked this Earth so many years
And I had known my share of tears
I'd stumbled through my former days
Most time was spent in lonely ways
Though I had known a lover's kiss
I'd never felt the utter bliss
That I now feel by loving you
And having you to love me too
An empty shell, one tenth a part
Of what would make me whole: a heart
And, thus, I walked around and 'round
Until, at last, I finally found
The missing nine tenths of my soul
And now I've found it makes me whole
You've finally come and filled me up
I'm now a shining, crystal cup
Not empty now, for your life fills
Me beyond my brim and over spills
The contents, beauty of our bliss
No more must I need sadly miss
Such pleasures as were meant for me
Through you my spirit is made free
You and I are now but one
Through us His Work may now be done

SET FREE

Through far-off lands, for many years
I've watched my life unfold
Too many times I'd tasted tears
In loneliness I strolled
I could not know there was a You
So, I just walked around
And misery my spirit knew
My eyes upon the ground
But then (Sweet Miracle!) did you
So suddenly appear
And in my life new meaning grew
No longer room for fear
You gave the greatest gifts to me
Just being in my world
You let me feel, and taste, and see
As our two bodies curled
And intertwining, joined as one
I was a man reborn
You cannot know what you have done
My life your love adorns
For now, my heart, my hopes held high
Within your arms in love
You lift my spirit to the sky
And now I live above
The former, lost and lonely me
No more; forever, now, set free

SWEET MOMENTS, DEAR

Now, as my little water craft
Gently nudges out from the pier
I remember how much we laughed
And shared the sweetest moments, Dear
Our lovely time together spent
As everywhere in love we went
And in each other's arms we shared
Our love and lust, our two hearts bared
We always share the greatest bliss
In greatest passion's rapture kiss
As Time stands still as our soul's meet
And merge as one, but one heart beat
You're mine, I'm yours, and eons spend
In love, and loving thus we blend
The greatest treasures pleasure's known
The seeds of purest passions sewn
But, now, as e'er we two must face
Between us come this little space
And as my little water craft
Allows the waves to wash the pier
I hold this thought of how we laughed
And shared those sweetest moments, Dear

WHAT LOVERS DO

A tear upon my cheek now streaks
You've been away these two long weeks
My heart is aching for your touch
And I am missing you so much
I now look back upon the time
When last we shared the most sublime
Of any love that e'er was felt
Between two souls as you did melt
Within my loving, tender touch
As I enjoyed your treasures much
And you, too, gave the greatest part
Of your sweet self, your loving heart
My lusty lips and tongue employed
So gently on you as I toyed
With parts of you so hot with fire
That night we shared such great desire
Just now, I can but reminisce
Remembering that deepest kiss
And, longing for your sweet embrace
I yearn to see your smiling face
When I can give my love to you
And we can do what lovers do

UPON THE SAND

We walk along, and, hand in hand
We leave our footprints in the sand
We stroll beside the high sand cliffs
In lover's thoughts our thinking drifts
As, to our left the ocean swells
And shuffles all the pretty shells
The briney mist thrown in the air
From whitecaps crashing everywhere
Upon the multicolored rock
That lines the winding path we walk
From time to time we pause to get
Another treasure into our net
Some spiral shell or rainbow rock
And as we do we also talk
About those things that brought us here
As your sweet lips I soon draw near
And warm and tender kiss we share
Eternal, blissful moments there
As we begin to feel the bliss
That lives within our love's sweet kiss
I soon reach out to take your hand
And lay you down upon the sand
Then while the crashing breakers roar
We share our love, our passions soar
And, surging as the ocean swells
Our love is made among the shells

That dot the sand along the shore
Our spirits with the seagulls soar
So many times we'll come back here
This loving spot we hold so dear
Each time these embers will be fanned
As love we share upon the sand

ANGEL

My mind drifts off and floats through Time
Midst thoughts and feelings so sublime
As you lay sleeping next to me
A lovely Angel do I see
You are so pretty laying there
I stroke your long, soft, golden hair
As I caress your rosey cheeks
A rainbow through your tresses streaks
You seem to glow from deep inside
When once with joy (though sleeping) sighed
Because you felt my tender touch
And it enhanced your dream so much
I lay so close, right next to you
And dream what I would love to do
If you awoke and saw me there
Playing gently with your hair
I dream that you would take my hand
And without words I'd understand
You feel the warmth and love, the fire
That burns for you, my great desire
You'd pull me down on top of you
As sparks were fanned as if you blew
Upon the embers in my heart
And stoking, stroking, you would start
To share your treasures as you gave
Yourself to me, your sweet love-slave

For countless hours we'd enjoy
Each other's bodies and employ
Those tender secrets we can share
As purest passions we do dare

NORTH WIND

Sometimes it gets too cold to snow
As cruel and bitter North Winds blow
And sun's rays hiding are not found
As crystals form now all around
Though trees are bare their branches wear
Such snowy sleeves and everywhere
Stand stark statues draped in white
The only contrast within sight
All other things a sea of snow
That hides all color deep below
Four feet now covers everything
And underneath the tree limbs cling
Long shards of ice formed days ago
When warmer skies did make them grow
It's minus twelve as North Winds race
Down through the canyons and erase
All traces of those little toes
That ran about on former snows
And for a while no snow will fall
Nor little creatures hither crawl
It's so damned cold it cannot snow
As long as these cruel North Winds throw
This icy breath through all the trees
As thinking even now does freeze

Soon to be published:
Of Sunlight And Shadows, Creative Arts
& Science Ent., July, 1997

INTO MY WORLD

To think that I had walked about
Those many years and done without
The simple pleasures I have found
As love now blossoms all around
I spent my life before we met
In trials and trouble and regret
So long I lived in dark despair
My happy moments were so rare
If I had known there was a you
My life would not have been so blue
But I saw not the Master's Plan
I was a most unhappy man
But when the time was then just right
You came anon, into my sight
A lovely angel from the clouds
And tore asunder all my shrouds
That I had worn for many years
And wiped away those useless tears
From that first day of my rebirth
My life had meaning and great worth
You brought to me such hope and joy
Life's sweet pleasures I now enjoy
And now I live my life in bliss
Enraptured by an Angel's kiss

GLORIOUS YOU

When I behold such pleasing scenes
Sometimes I ponder what it means
To view the world in such a light
Each thing a wonder to my sight
Each way I look, each thing I view
A nice reflection, only you
I see a beauty in **all** things
Such peacefulness your spirit brings
Since first you came into my space
I was entranced by your sweet face
But, soon, I found your spirit there
Waiting, patient, longing to share
The greatest joys a man can know
And these, then, gladly did you show
So, now that you have been revealed
To knowledge of you I now yield
And I don't wonder anymore
How, or why, as I did before
I just cherish each sweet minute
Of your grace and live within it
For, there is nothing else that brings
Such utter joy as my heart sings
These tributes to glorious you
In thanks, for love, and all you do

YOUR LOVE I SEE

Your lines I've heard, devoid of rhyme
Yet, portraits painted are sublime
Such special thoughts with pen you write
Reflected visions a delight
Your dreams and hopes and love you say
In such a soft and gentle way
With words you've chosen just for me
Through these sweet lines your love I see

LOVE SET FREE

As ink on pages starts to spill
My thoughts begin to drive my quill
My mind recalls that special day
When first your words of love did play
Upon my heart and echo there
And tender feelings you did share
Across Life's many miles you brought
Your loving presence as you taught
Me Life's sweet joys and certain bliss
Those warm sensations in your kiss
Enchained, my soul your love now grips
As you enslave me with your lips
And send my spirit into space
With tenderness and love erase
My former, lonely, empty world
Within your loving arms now curled
You brought me hope and strength and joy
As love's great powers you employ
In bringing sweet relief to me
By loving you, my love's set free

THEE

As you prepare to come to me
These thoughts I want to give to thee:
I have now waited these long weeks
Denied the pleasures my love seeks
For, in thee's absence I was such
A worthless man who missed thee much
Who lived in darkness, without grace
An empty shell, a basket case
I could hold on to thoughts of thee
Those times thee had last set me free
From pains I felt before I knew
Such pleasures found in things thee do
By tender, deep, and secret touch
Those things I've grown to love so much
For these are greatest pleasures sent
As ever True Love's passions spent
Themselves between two lovers' hearts
Our hearts both pierced by Cupid's darts
So, now, as thee prepare to come
In loving thoughts of thee I hum
This little song so thee may hear
These words of Love, for thee, my Dear

HEART ON FIRE

These words cannot do justice to
My deep, abiding love for you
How can a man express the bliss
Contained within a single kiss?
With words how can he hope to write
The joys he feels within the light
Of your sweet presence, soft and fair
Or of the perfume of your hair?
How can a man attempt to show
The special ways you let him know
You were designed and sent to him
And fill his heart beyond the brim?
Though verse and rhyme I may employ
They can't describe the perfect joy
You give to me just being near
Or, having you to love me, Dear
For these, mere words, cannot express
The tender love in your caress
Nor ecstasy within your touch
No words could ever do so much
And, so, I do not try to say
In words what's on my mind today
I shall just cherish all day through
The love I long to share with you
And when you have come home to me
No words I'll need for you to see
My perfect love, my great desire
And how you've set my heart on fire

ALASKAN WINTER SURVIVAL KIT

For many months now we have stayed
In little cabins, as children played
In mountains of this Winter's white
That buries everything from sight
The Summer's roaming Tourist's gone
Now, prob'ly sits upon his lawn
And sips iced tea and tans his bod
In Summer climes and thinks how odd
That we have stayed here in the cold
Where not a drop of iced tea's sold
So, gift shops close and business stops
And we to little cabins go
Our lonely respite from the snow
While we stay cooped within these walls
We mumble as more fresh snow falls
We soon begin to babble, too
So long in boredom did we view
The only thing within our sight
That boring, blasted, frozen white
Till Spring's next thaw we will be stuck
With thumbs in mouths, content to suck
Upon that thing that pulls us through
These boring Winters stuck with you
What survivors of these Winters require
The "Cabin Fever Reliever Pacifier"

BRIGHT STAR

I had been searching for so long
And wandered, lost, among the throng
Among the multitude, alone
Within my world no bright star shone
I'd travelled over far-off lands
And stood on many beaches' sands
I'd heard the rolling oceans' sigh
And watched great, soaring eagles fly
I'd conquered lofty mountain peaks
And viewed such dazzling sunset streaks
I'd sailed upon the seven seas
And tasted every briney breeze
That rushed upon a distant shore
Or, through a coral reef did roar
I'd been where snowdrifts pile so high
And ageless treetops touch the sky
I'd seen such wonders of this Earth
And witnessed Death, as well as Birth
I'd seen such things in my life's quest
And yet, I never would have guessed
That, while I searched the whole world through
In truth, I really searched for you
And, finding you, I know you are
My quest fulfilled, my life's Bright Star

Soon to be published:
Of Sunlight And Shadows, Creative Arts &
Science Ent., July 1997
American Poetry Annual, The Amherst Society, 1997

A THOUSAND LINES

In loneliness my heart has pined
One thousand lines to you designed
My loving thoughts in verse was written
Expressing how my heart was smitten
These visions of you, so terrific
Make this Poet most prolific
As I remain, lost deep in thought
Reflecting on the joys you brought
Into my world since you came in
And our sweet loving did begin
Though you are many miles away
And for this little time must stay
So far from tender, loving me
I'll hold you close and faithfully
Adore the visions in my mind
Our loving souls again entwined
Those greatest pleasures that I miss
When I'm denied your lips to kiss
So, I shall hold these thoughts of you
Of all the things I yearn to do
When you return and we may find
Sweet dreams come true that I designed
The thousand verses that I wrote
As love for you I did devote

LOVE LETTERS

So many letters did I send
As you became my dearest friend
Because we could not be united
(By many miles were we divided)
We courted for a while by letter
And got to know each other better
As knowledge of your spirit grew
I could not help myself, for you
So swiftly to my heart had eased
And there onto my heartstrings seized
For many weeks we were content
While courtship was through letters sent
But then, at last, could writing end
And though you would remain my friend
By coming home to be with me
You also would my lover be
And now, because you were my friend
Because of many letters penned
So long ago across those miles
In every way, with joy, and smiles
Your friend, **and** lover will I be
From now and through eternity

THE TELEPHONE

You called last night and filled me in
On what you'd done and how you've been
And once again your love did send
Across the miles we must pretend
That you are not so far away
And that you came back home today
Imagining your sweet embrace
And, laying with you, face to face
As warmth we trade, our bodies bare
While tender love and dreams we share
We fantasize upon the phone
And in this way our love has grown
Because we've talked of things I'll do
When, once again, I can love you
In ways rehearsed while you were gone
In lovers' grasp from dusk to dawn
I'll live my dreams, at last made true
These dreams created just for you
And though these days the phone has been
The closest contact we have seen
Thank God for those sweet thoughts designed
To get us through while two hearts pined
For, soon, you will be home with me
And passions from our dreams set free

FRIENDS

As I sit here, though I'm alone
I'm thinking of great friends I've known
Although, as hermit, I now live
Sweet reverie these friendships give
The pain of solitude would tend
To hurt, if I could not depend
On thoughts of what these friendships bring
And, so, I sit remembering
The faces of these dear, sweet friends
As though they're here, my mind pretends
From friendships made so long ago
Rekindled now and all aglow
The greatest treasure of them all
In this life there is no equal
To comfort found within the mind
In knowing how such friendships bind
Two souls, though very far away
Together will they ever stay
So, when I start to feel alone
I think of those great friends I've known
And, cherishing sweet thoughts, I sing
This song of love these friendships bring

TWO HEARTS

Do not mind that I love you so
My love for you is all I know
There is, for me, no greater thing
This sweetest joy with love you bring
You need to know how long I'd sought
Elusive love and why I thought
I would not ever know the bliss
Within your touch, or tender kiss
Until you came and let me feel
Your love, and secrets you reveal
I did not know such joys could be
Contained within your love for me
Or mine for you, as we now show
Two hearts made hot, as passions glow

TONE DEAF

Melodious marching
Wordless
Without meaning or import
Trampling across the face of my mind
Left no emotions moved
Nor heart strings strung
Nor cymbals clanging hope
Nor enchanting echoes resounding
Strings of insignificant notes
Held together by meaningless
Soundless syllabic muttering
Giving meaning to the multitude
But, lost to deaf ears
That could not hear
The beauty of music
Until you

RAGS TO RICHES

Not knowing you were there
So long ago
I'd given up on love
Resigned to my solitude
Blind to joys of life
Ignorant of bliss
Not knowing what I missed
As happy as I knew how
Yet, a pauper
Content with meager fruits
Crumbs of satisfaction
Oblivious to rewards designed
So long ago
Not allowed to see
Rich treasures hoarded
A priceless trove prepared
Now makes me King
Above all things
Knowing you are here
Having you so near
Loving you, my Dear

SEEDS OF PASSION

I

I've written lots of verse in rhyme
And measured metric thought sublime
A thousand verses have I penned
And over many miles did send
The thoughts and feelings you have made
While, with my heartstrings you have played
Though you could not be here with me
These visions of you that I see
Make time go by until you're here
And I can love you so, my Dear
Then, when you have come home at last
I run to greet you, and, so fast
We're in each other's arms once more
And I'm with the one I do adore

II

Those visions, useless now, faded
For sweet sight of you were traded
Now, as I hold you to me tight
I'm squeezing you into the night
And, cherishing your tender heart
Such hot lovemaking we do start
Our passions ready, burning red
Entwined, two bodies soon are led
Into the realm of purest bliss

Enjoying lovers' deepest kiss
Then, taking turns, give greatest joys
These special secrets love employs
You fondle me, I play with you
And everything with love we do

III

This eon spent, together, there
While trading such sweet love we dare
To stop the hands of Father Time
As, to the clouds two spirits climb
And float in joy, our hearts set free
Enraptured with such ecstasy
Our love, so pure, we can be sure
Through the ages it will endure
And grow and blossom more and more
As through the clouds our hopes may soar
Eternal, great, this love we share
Reflections of a perfect pair
The purest love that e'er was grown
From tender seeds of passions sewn

LOVE TRANSCENDS

Mere words will ever fail me
God knows how hard I've tried
To paint a portrait of my love
Each time left with only lines and dots
Clutter upon the page
Inadequate, unintelligible
Meaningless drivel
Boring, borrowed cliches
My love transcends language
For, words cannot express
And only make trite
Feelings that remain
Beyond literary expression
I can show these deep feelings
Emotions born of my love
Yearnings from deep within my heart
I can show you the color
The texture, and composition
Meter and rhyme
The sonorous beauty
Of my magnificent love for you
But I shall ever fail to convince you
By silly words I write or say
So, please don't make me fail
Abusing language

And my heart
With mere words
Make me succeed
Leave me free to create my masterpiece
A pure, perfect reflection
Demonstrative proof
Where words do not exist
Unnecessary in that universe
As I show my love for you

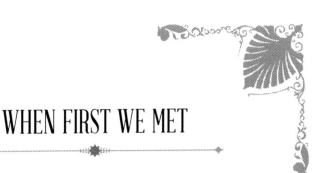

WHEN FIRST WE MET

I

When first we met
Love came fast
There was no time to dance
Or date, or fool around
For, by the time we met
Our hearts were already ripe
Ready for the picking
And fruits fell from the vine
Without urging
Sweet, yielding love

II

When first we met
Though, across many miles
So unorthodox
Two hot hearts
Super-magnetic
Drew each other in
Grasping and holding
Never to relinquish
Two, before alone
Strong together now as one

III

When first we met
You reached out to me
And let me into your world
I fit so nicely there
As though that empty space
That existed in your world
Was a reflection of all that I am
The missing half of you
And I filled it all up
Like air rushing into a vacuum

IV

When first we met
Though searching
We had never hoped to find
A kindred spirit
Soul Mate
True Love
Lover
And Friend
Too great to be true
Until we found each other

V

When first we met
Love and Life became easy
And so much fun
The trial and burden
Curse of loneliness
And eternity of pain
We had known so long
Vaporized, as though
It had never existed
And our only memory was Love

VI

When first we met
Our love was dizzying
Rapturous
Too wonderful to believe
Until we remembered
Such are the miracles
Planned and put in motion
The twitch of a finger
As mountains are moved
By our sweet Lord

VII

When first we met
Love came so fast
Neither you, nor I
Could have been prepared
Caught by surprise
Incredulous
Reeling from sudden bliss
Inflamed with the ecstasy
Yet, cautious and afraid
Doubting reality

VIII

When first we met
Our hopes and dreams
Wildest fantasies fulfilled
We could not deny the truth
As our two souls joined
And we admitted to joys
Receiving hungrily
Exchanging passions unleashed
Letting loose our love
Surrendering to our lust

IX

When we first met
We could not fathom
That boundless
Eternal
Blissful love
That rocked our world
Sending our spirits
Wafting high
Euphoric
Free at last

ALL OF YOU

In life there's good and stormy weather
And, though I may not have you forever
Every moment, now, while I do
I can't help wanting all of you
I know I promised unconditional love
As if I could measure and control
The expression of my heart's desire
Hold back the flames of passion's fire
Forgive me, Dear, I could not know
Beyond restraint my love would grow
And know no bounds, nor chains could hold
As passions for you did unfold
So, though I tried to leave you free
Not hold too tight or ever be
Possessive or expect too much
Since I have known your tender touch
I cannot help myself and now
In pieces fall my broken vow
I tried so hard, I never meant
To break my word, till I was sent
By Love, beyond the mortal world
And to the place of gods was hurtled
But I, not god of anything
Succumb to pleasures that you bring
Weak and helpless, I cannot hold
My passions back, so, I'm made bold
And through good, and stormy weather
Though I can't have you forever
Every moment, now, while I do
I can't help wanting all of you!

YOU!

Thinking, **feeling** my love for you
In sweet repose, I transcend myself
Gently rocking, as a suckling babe
Nestling at its mother's breast
Dreamily swinging, as the pendulum
That is a small water craft
Dipping up and down between the swells
Melodic, surge and crash, ensuing renewal
And cleansing with each rhythmic beat
Of the ocean's pulse on endless sands
Softly singing, gentle breathing
The voice of the wind through the trees
Rapturous sounds of suns setting
Crisp crackling of colorful streaks of dawn
Listing, listening, able to discern
Sounds within sounds
Formally opaque and unheard
Now, tumultuous, droning
Beating of birds' wings
And drops of tiny foot pods
As propagation pushes forth
The flowers blooming
Hear leaves and petals unfurl
Exposing Nature's nakedness
Aware!
Aware!

Alive, and in tune with all things
Alive!
Reborn
Awakened
Harmonious
Affinity of souls established
Contentment
You

WHEN LOVE WAS BORN

Through so many quiet moments
We talked and laughed
Sharing our thoughts and feelings
Having fun together
Enjoying the exciting discovery
Of each other
It was during these early times
In our remarkable, wonderful relationship
When, sharing our innermost secrets
And desires
And fantasies for our lives
That we bared our souls
Each letting the other into their world
Touching hearts
And becoming one spirit
It is then that Love was born
And it was then
Such a tender, beautiful love
Became the link in the chain
Between our two hearts
And minds
Unbreakable and eternal
It was in this infancy of our love
We learned amazing things
That our love had been planned

And set in motion
Long ago
That all of our previous days
Some good, some not so good
Were just preparation for the bliss
Realized during the awakening of our love
That earth-shaking blossoming and bearing
Of sweet fruits
That ours would prove to be
A love so great and strong
And right
We could not deny it
No more than we could
Fathom its magnificence
For, it exceeds all other
Making every breath
Rejuvenation
Every second
A long stroll through Paradise
Every thought and sight
A wonder
And every song
A love song
But, the most amazing thing
As we laid the stones of the foundation
Of our sweet love

In these early days
When Time stood still for us
Was the realization
That, by giving in to our love
We were fulfilling our destinies
Making our whole life right
By loving each other
We really were loving ourselves
For, we came to understand
Though miles may have come between us
We have always been a part of each other
And we are now complete
Fulfilled and content
To the extent we have surrendered
To the control, and demands
And splendor
Of our love for each other

WITHIN YOUR ARMS

Now, what have you done?
What, between us, has begun?
Did you really mean to start
This great beating of my heart?
You came, you are
And will ever be
The same bright star
Source of all my glee
You are the focus of my desire
Your sweet love sets me on fire
And, burning, craving you so much
Longing, yearning for your touch
Wishing I could devour you
And you would ravish me too
I cannot help but think of bliss
That comes within your sweet kiss
And things we'll do when I can be
Again within your arms set free

MISERY

Since you cannot be here today
And for a little while must stay
Beyond my reach, beyond my touch
I'm sad, and missing you so much
The pain's so real, the hurt's so deep
Your absence makes these tears I weep
Within my mind I see your face
As I recall our last embrace
When lips were locked within that kiss
That lingers as I reminisce
The sight, the smell, the warmth of you
Sensations, hints of love we knew
When you were here and held me tight
And we made love into the night
That's all I have while I remain
Without your sweet love once again
So, Lover, please come back to me
Come home and end my misery
I'm so depressed without you here
And my heart's yearning for you, Dear

TRIBUTE TO ALASKA
[ALASKA THRILLS]

Because Alaska's home to me
And since I've lived in this great land
In verses Heaven's bliss I see
And marvel at the Grace God planned
A tribute to this land I sing
Where glacial rivers winding bring
Huge Pinks, and Reds, and Kings to spawn
In places men have never gone
White peaks pierce clouds where eagles soar
And deep through canyons North winds roar
Like rows of soldiers White Birch stand
So tall and straight and give this land
A special beauty all its own
Where many treasures great are grown
Though briefly Summer Season stays
While here, upon the tundra lays
The Fireweed in raging reds
On hillsides burning carpet spreads
Rich indigo of Lupine plants
Beneath clear azure skies entrance
Dwarf Dogwood and the Devil's Club
A rainbow graces every shrub
Lush Cranberries in high bush form
When ripe, like bees, great Grizzlies swarm

Great Ferns and Mushrooms grow so high
With trees and mountains touch the sky
And, bursting forth with Nature's powers
This tapestry of Summer flowers
Each way I look, each thing I see
Such beauty brings me ecstasy
While roaming over Heaven's hills
Enthralled by such Alaskan thrills

NIGHTSCAPE

You make the hands of Time stand still
These visions of you such a thrill:
You brighten darkness in the night
The moon a sun within my sight
The stars are diamonds hanging high
From twilight's gown, a sequined sky
Great comets streaking out in space
Unseen, unheard, they swiftly race
Until they burst into the air
Like brilliant sunbeams through your hair
Those brightest stars, that light the skies
Glimmer and glisten like your eyes
So, while I stare into the night
I'm awed by darkness, and by light
Entranced by wonders out in space
Each one a feature of your face
Where Beauty reigns, a happy Queen
And you're that beauty I have seen

Published
The Best Poems Of The 90's,
National Library of Poetry
Our World's Favorite Poems, World Of Poetry
Soon to be published in:
Poetic Voices of America,
Sparrowgrass Poetry Forum, Inc.
October 15, 1996

SNOW SONG

Cold, cumulous clouds
come creeping
clinging

Taunting
teasing
tearing tops of twisted trees

Brutish brisk breeze
blasting
bringing

Fall's first flakes
furious flurry
flying freeze

Season's sacred sea
silhouetted
silent snow

Weighty wardrobe
wrapped around
Winter's white

Bending Birch boughs
buried
below

Sparkling
spectacle
such sweet sight!

THE NINE DAUGHTERS

With Father, Zeus, that noble King
In chorus do nine daughters sing
Melodic voices, pleasing, sweet
Uplifting, sit at Father's feet
And on Olympus do follow
Such wise guidance from Apollo
Young and fair through eons, singing
Revealing hopes the future's bringing
Showing men a new tomorrow
Banishing all grief and sorrow
These nine sit and await your call
Prepared to lift you and enthrall
Your spirits in such lofty lines
And help creative verse designs
Each one her own skill addresses
Essence of that Art possesses
For writing Epic poetry
Just call upon Calliope
Or, if you wish to write of love
Erato waits for you above
Euterpe with all Lyric rhyme
Will help, while teaching thought sublime
To write of a dark, tragic scene
You'll want to call on Melpomene
Clio helps write Historic facts
While Thalia with Comedic Acts

And if you write of Stars and Space
Urania will your thinking grace
Polyhymnia is the one
To seek when sacred song's begun
Then, last but not least, is Terpsichore
Who's magic dances set you free
Thus, each of these Nine Daughters sing
For you, and closer to their Father bring
Your thoughts and verse and helps you write
Those lofty lines that shine the Light
So all of Mankind sees the way
To Truth and Beauty and may stay
In joy from what your verse has shown
With help from nine daughters you've known

POETIC ADORATION

You are so great, I thought I'd write
This tribute to my thoughts of you
Since first you came into my sight
And of great passions that I knew.

My pen can't help but spill forth rhyme
For, ink flows quickly into song
As words paint pictures so sublime
And glorify for whom I long.

The knowledge of what your love brings
Creates such feeling in my heart
And of that Love this heart now sings
Until this Poet's done his part.

Thus, thought of You are all I use
To cause my words to so inspire
Assistance from Erato, Muse
Of Romance, Love, Passion, Desire.

And, driven thus, these lines sing of
My adoration and ring true
A testimony to my love
And devotion to only You.

Published in Outstanding Poets of 1994,
The National Library Of Poetry, 1994

O! SPRINGTIME!

O! Springtime! Blazing ball of fire
Nature's awesome morning empire
Warm rays dance on every tree
With rapid rising mercury
Hush of silent night departing
As nocturnals daydreams starting
This new day to life is bringing
Great trees, and bees, and birds singing
Though snow's still deep on every hill
Warm sun's urging makes rivers fill
As, faster toward the sea they flow
Snow's leaving lets sweet new life grow
While, warmer skies and longer days
Make miracles in wondrous ways
O! Springtime makes all things alive
These woods and glens where creatures thrive
Now, bursting forth, this vibrant scene
As landscapes change from white to green
And rainbows spill onto the land
O! Springtime spreads such pleasures grand

LOOK WHAT YOU DID TO ME

You came along, from far beyond my world
And expectations
Entering a lonely, empty space
Filling me with resurrected hopes
Spawning blissful dreams
Kindling buried passions, unexpected, undeserved
Yet, in answer to all prayers
Soon promised life fulfilled
And gave those missing parts
(Before I'd been but half a man)
Then, between two blinkings of my eyes
You made me whole, complete
A better man by far than what I was
Alone, before you came into my world
But then you left me
Brokenhearted once again

ACROSS TIME AND SPACE

Though Time and Space did come between
Two souls and different paths had seen
The sep'rate footprints of their feet
N'er would have guessed these two would meet
She'd gone her way; so too, had he
Until such time when there could be
A gentle merging of their ways
Where two hearts warmed by one sun's rays
Who could have known, who might have thought
Great Time and Distance matter not?
For, new found feelings transcend Space
And eons passed these now replace
And other feelings warm and new;
Your thoughts of him, his dreams of you

WHY MUST YOU BE SO FAR AWAY?

I'm sitting here, alone today
Why must you be so far away?
The tragedy of Life is this:
My lips are longing for your kiss
And arms now yearn for your embrace
And eyes for sight of your sweet face

You have become so much to me
Your loveliness is all I see
When my mind's eye envisions you
As now it oft is wont to do

For, here I sit within the gloom
Alone within this little room
And wonder when you will be here
So I can hold you close, my Dear

Thus, thoughts and visions are my fare
While I am here, and you are there
These dreams, these hopes, sweet memory
Are all I have, 'cept agony
I'm sitting here, alone today
Why must you be so far away?

MY SPECIAL FRIEND

Our friendship's precious and so new
I cannot help but dream of you
In days <u>and</u> nights my thoughts return
To you, my sweet, and thus I yearn
To once again enjoy that bliss
That's found within one gentle kiss

We haven't known each other long
But two hearts sing a happy song
For we have grown so close of late
And now share feelings deep and great

We give each other many thrills
With hopes and dreams our future fills
So, your sweet face and gentle heart
Are all I see as Cupid's dart
Takes hold of me and makes knees weak
Those lovely visions all I seek

Just now, I cherish every thought
Of every feeling you have brought
With special friendship that we know
As more in love with you I grow

DAWNSORROW

I sit and stare as stars of night
So quickly disappear from sight.
Those yellow moonbeams also fade
From landscapes where last night they played

Now, as the sun begins to rise
It warms, and brightens Eastern skies
And with this early morning light
To guide my pen I start to write.

I'm moved by thoughts that came when sleep
Denied from me did make me weep.
So troubled was my mind with fear
Because you were not here, my Dear.

When you are close you soothe my pain
Just like the gentle morning rain
That washes clean the dusty ground
While, in your loving arms I'm found.

But, now, such torture I endure!
Each night without you I am sure
Will take its awful toll on me
And I will know this misery!

MY DESIRE

Your lovely face entrances me
Again, the sweetest sight I see
Those magic eyes, your sexy lips
Such perfect lines as my mind grips
And holds these visions of such grace
Contained in features of your face

Your gentle words uplifting me
Again, to heights of ecstasy
The things you say, and things you share
'bout dreams you've had and hopes you dare
Such special, blissful feelings bring
To me, and cause my heart to sing

Your soft caress is shaking me
Again, you set my passions free
And ways you know, and things you show
With fire does your sweet love glow
Your tender touch makes my soul fly
Away, up into clouds so high

Your passions, hot, are burning me
But, burning would I rather be
Than if you were not in my arms
Dissolving all my pain with charms
Dancing in that magic fire
Fanning flames of my desire

Soon to be published:
Of Sunlight And Shadows, Creative Arts And Science Ent., July 1997
Sensations, Iliad Press, 1997
Quill Books, 1997

GOD'S GIFT TO ME

Despite five-thousand miles between
Two souls, a love as ne'er was seen
Soon born of hopes and dreams has grown
And now our hearts this love have known.

Despite the pains and tears we knew
As hopeless though we sometimes grew
In loneliness and misery
Until, at last, you came to me.

We had been lost, left pleasureless
So long denied the tenderness
That flows so pure from Heaven's spring
And to our hearts great treasures bring.

All pain and hurt is chased away
Forevermore we now will stay
In world of bliss, eternal, free
Such is the love you've brought to me.

Because I know how great God is
I know, your love, a gift of His
To me, so rare and pure, so fine
I'll always cherish; it's divine.

MERE WORDS

Dear Heart, so many times I've tried
To say what's buried deep inside
So many times I've tried to say
In words what's on my mind today
But words cannot begin to show
The feelings I'm now blessed to know
Since you began to care for me
And since your sweet love set me free
My Love, mere words cannot express
The bliss I find in your caress
The tender caring of your touch
The gentle touch I love so much
I've written lines of love before
But what I feel for you is more
Than written words can ever say
So, silent, still, my pen will stay
Useless here within my hand
And, meager words that I had planned
Pass through my mind and go unsaid
Not written, never to be read
Mere words, no longer meet the test
Nor show the love with which I'm blessed
Since you began to care for me
And since your sweet love set me free

Soon to be published:
Of Sunlight And Shadows, Creative Arts
And Science Ent., July, 1997

JUST FOR ME

When God began to form the Earth
He planned each man's and woman's birth
And thought about good things He'd give
To these, all people who would live
Within the Garden He conceived
And how these gifts would be received
God knows all things and so He knew
So long ago, there'd be a You
Who'd come along to ease the strife
That I would know within my life.
He knew so long ago I'd see
In time, the bliss you'd bring to me
Just being you, and that you'd bring
Me joys of which great Poets sing
He knew, because He planned all this
Ensuring I would know the bliss
Within my lifetime, and, would see
You were created just for me . . .

FLOWERS JUST FOR YOU

A flower is a precious thing
Where early morning dew did cling
And bees in tiny circles flew
Before 't was plucked and sent to you

This flow'ry group so long was grown
While fragrance sweet was skyward blown
And beauty stored in petals then
I'm sure will make you smile again

Though life is fragile, it is sweet
And flowers are a special treat
They grow and blossom a short while
Their beauty's made to make you smile

Though flowers plucked so soon will fade
And off to rest these soon are laid
Enjoy the beauty and the scent
While here. For you these joys were meant

EVENING'S STORM

With Summer's passing my heart heaves
As raging fire spreads through the leaves.
Ablaze with color sway the trees
Pushed to and fro by gentle breeze.
A brilliant light show hurts my eyes
As lightning streaks the evening skies.
Bright traces burn into my brain
And signal of the coming rain.
But, first the rolling thunder comes
And pounds the air like kettle drums.
It rumbles o'er these wooded hills
And with great joy my spirit fills.
Then, soon enough the raindrops pound
Into the trees and on the ground.
As gentle patter they begin
But stir emotions deep within.
I sit and watch these storms go by
So thrilled by magic in the sky
And marvel at these sights and sounds
Where awesome beauty here abounds!

Published in: A Break In The Clouds,
National Library Of Poetry, 1993

DREAMS COME TRUE

As I reflect on times gone by
I think of ways I felt before
Before I knew the How and Why
And reached these heights through which I soar

Though I had known a tender kiss
I could not know that I would be
So far beyond that realm of bliss
When your sweet lips would set me free

Though I had known a loving touch
I dared not dream that there would be
A touch I'd grow to love so much
And what your touch would do to me

Though I had known successes, too
I could not feel triumphant then
But now, in everything I do
Through you, I triumph, once, again

Though life before had shown me joy
Because I could not know that you
Such loving powers would employ
You've made my greatest dreams come true!

ETERNAL LOVE

I want to give you the kind of love
That will win your whole heart
So that I can be the center of your universe
As you are mine
I want to be your dearest friend
One you want to share everything with
One to support and care for you
As only your dearest friend could
I want to be your red-hot lover
To share the secret ecstasy
Only you and I will know
As we give all of ourselves to each other
I want to win your heart
To capture you
Tame you
Guide you to new heights of joy
But, more than anything else
I want your happiness
I want what's good for you
So, as I capture you
I set you free
As I tame you
I leave you wild and unhindered
And, as I guide you
You guide me
Hand in hand
In love
Loving
From now and to Eternity

SWEET RELEASE

Again, you are so far away
But now I will not sit here sad
This time I know you will not stay
And through your happiness I'm glad

You needed this: a trip back East
Where family now can shower you
With tenderness that's been increased
By time and distance you all knew

You've not been home in seven years
At Christmastime and that's a shame
But now, shed naught but happy tears
For absence <u>you</u> are not to blame

Forget that shackles kept you here
You're home and that's what really counts
Soak up the love you hold most dear
Forget all else as your joy mounts

So, here's my wish across these miles
A wish to show my love is true:
I wish you happiness and smiles
And nothing but the best for you

I am not selfish, so I give
My blessings for your trip back East
Your happiness is why I live
All shackles now have been released

SINCE YOU HAVE COME INTO MY WORLD

So many years ('t was twenty three)
Since last I'd seen your lovely face
Or since you'd sweetly smiled at me
Such long, cruel years I would replace
If I could re-write History . . .
I would have held you tenderly

So long ago I missed the chance
To know the bliss your love would bring
These joys I now feel in one glance
From you, that makes my whole heart sing
And leaves me in hypnotic trance
As I in ecstasy now dance

I'm glad you came into my world
Though Time was meant to run its course
For, now, within your arms I'm curled
Of all my joys you are the source
And pleasures never dreamed unfurled
Since you have come into my world

HOLDING YOU IN LOVING THOUGHT

Because you're on my mind today
And in my heart, though far away
I'm holding you in loving thought
For all the joys that you have brought
Into my life and for the glee
Your precious love has given me
So, as I sit and think of you
I'm awed by how our sweet love grew
Not long ago across the miles
And how this love brings many smiles
For, though you must be far away
You're in my loving arms today!

IN LOVE WITH YOU TILL END OF TIME

In Nineteen-Sixty-Nine your face
Upon my mind last left its trace
In other time and other place
I first was stricken by your grace
But, eons passed devoid of glee
And many dark days did I see
While you were far away from me
Fulfilling your own destiny
I waited long, so many years
Left lost and hopeless by my fears
And blinded by my lonely tears
Until, at last, true love appears
I thought that I had lived before
Since I had heard great oceans roar
And seen such mighty eagles soar
And watched cascading rivers pour
By love I thought I too had flown
To heights of joy from passions known
But love I'd felt had never shown
Such bliss the seeds of your love's grown
For I'd not known a love so real
Nor passions, bliss, or lovers' zeal
Nor that your sweet love would reveal
The peace my aching heart could feel
At last, in Nineteen-Ninety-Two

My greatest dreams in life came true
From far away, out of the blue
Our unexpected friendship grew
That friendship was a precious thing
But soon much more to us would bring
For, out of friendship love would spring
And our two hearts as one would sing
So, as I sit and write this rhyme
And up to greater heights I climb
I'm feeling sweetest bliss sublime
In love with you till end of Time

CHRISTMAS IN KENTUCKY

Though ice and snow are falling down
Upon this West Kentucky town
This Christmas day is clear and bright
And everything's a joyous sight!

An unexpected Winter storm
Makes flying snowflakes quickly form
And, in the wind, without a sound
These throw a blanket on the ground.

The trees and shrubs are such a sight
A trace of brown, but mostly white
Make branches look like silken sleeves
Where snow now grows in place of leaves.

There's nothing like a virgin snow
On Christmas Day to make hearts glow
But this is one to top them all
So heavenly as snowflakes fall!

THE PRECIOUS GIFTS OF CHRISTMAS

In honor of this Christmas Day
We pause with praise to God and say
Our thanks for blessings He has sent
To us, and for great joys He meant
For us to feel through knowledge of
The gifts He sent to show His love.
There are no gifts beneath our tree
Or fancy things for you and me
That came in boxes or with bows.
We do not have a need for those
Because we have the special things
The knowledge of His Sweet Love brings
In counting gifts He sent to please us
The first, the greatest: Christ Jesus
Who lived and died so long ago
So in our lifetime we would know
True Grace, forgiveness, and could be
Through Him, in joy and ecstasy
The second gift, with Love He gave
So we need never fear the grave
And though one day we'll draw no breath
We need not have a fear of death
For, through the first, from death He frees us
To share Eternity with Jesus.
The last, of these most precious gifts
By which our spirits He uplifts:
The special Love that we now know

As more in love each day we grow
So blessed while we are living here
Until, at last, He draws us near.
We are so blessed and, so we raise
Our voice in song and hands in praise
And on this special Christmas Day
We pause to thank Him and to say
Some special words for all the things
Just loving one another bringd

SONG OF LOVE

Here is a song I sing for you
Its melody is soft and light
About how love from sadness grew
Though dark in part, it leaves moods bright.
I wrote this song to soothe your mind
In times like this when you may doubt
If you were ever meant to find
True Love. This song is all about
The lives we led before we met
And sadness that we both went through.
But, sadness we must not regret
For, out of it our sweet love grew.
And now, I'll start this soothing rhyme;
Sit back and let it touch your soul.
I pray, through it, your spirits climb . . .
Your happiness my only goal:

For many years were dreams denied
And silent, bitter tears we cried
While we both felt within our souls
Our lives were not fulfilling goals
That we had set when very young
And onto which great hopes we'd hung
So, we endured those many years
Near drowning in our silent tears
We suffered quietly so long
Though we knew something must be wrong

And while we lived in misery
Beyond our pain we could not see
We'd given up and lost all hope
Resigned, defeated, tried to cope
With what we thought was meant to be
The best life held for you and me
So lost within the pain we knew
We could not see the Love that grew
From seeds we'd planted in our past
And that these seeds would bloom at last
Oh! What a flower blossomed then
And brought great hope to us again!
Its fragrant petals are so rare
And send sweet scents into the air!
A joy, of sights and feelings, too
Erases all the pains we knew
For this sweet flower makes hearts fly
And Love it brings will never die
Its magic beauty I sing of
For, through this magic we found Love
And though we waited long for this
We now, together, know the bliss
That comes with Love's eternal power
Grown ripe within this precious Flower
So, as the harvest we now reap
We share a love so true and deep
And never more will we know tears
For True Love blooms throughout the years!

LOVE SONGS IMMORTAL

With lines of verse, in couplets rhymed
Onto poetic heights I've climbed
And sat among great Muses where
Our voices sent into the air
Such songs, and tribute to my love . . .
Now, once again, this song sings of
The sweetest bliss I've ever known
And just how great that love has grown
Without the blessings of a Muse
Less lofty would be words I'd choose
And never could I hope to find
A way to show what's on my mind
That pays the tribute that is due
Or truly serves to honor you
Immortal, fine, my words can be
When Muses choose to sit with me
And help me find the perfect rhyme
Eternal tribute throughout Time
So, when I'm blessed to sit on high
With Muses, while, with verse I try
To glorify and honor you
My great poetic dreams come true
Then, words I write and songs I sing
Immortalize the love you bring
Into my life by being you
And by the great things that you do

MORNING GLORY

As this day's beauty starts to flower
I show my awe within this story
A tribute to our dear Lord's power
So all may see His lasting glory

As Mother Nature's gears now shift
From tranquil night to busy day
Nocturnals off to sleep soon drift
While, all the rest come out to play

As owls and nighttime creatures yawn
And snuggle into daytime beds
With coming new day's gentle dawn
The sleepy others raise their heads

As early morning light reveals
The shapes of last night's fleeting dreams
Those sunbeams brighten Life's ideals
And in this light my spirit beams

As tiny dewdrops all around
Make magic prisms in this light
A million rainbows on the ground
Enhance this morning's pleasing sight

As I enjoy each new day's grace
My heart's made happy and I see
Within reflections our Lord's face
And each day brings me ecstasy!

Published in: Best poems Of 1996,
National Library Of Poetry, 1996
Soon to be published:
Sensations, Iliad Press, 1997
A Treasury Of Verse, JMW Publishing, 1997

MY FATHER IS NEVER TOO BUSY FOR ME

My Father is always very, very busy
He was very busy this morning . . .
Shaping little fingers and toes
And breathing Sweet Life
Into a few million newborn babes,
Moving a few mountains around
Making the Wind and Seas and Stars
Go to where He wanted them to be,
Making sure the Sun and Moon
Would rise and fall right on schedule;
Shaking the Earth in a few spots
Just to keep things interesting.
Yes, today, as on all mornings
My Father was very, very busy
When I called His Name.
But, as always, He was true to His Promise
And when I called His Name this morning
He immediately dropped what He was doing
And came down from on High,
Sat down beside me,
Listened to what I had to say,
And we prayed together
And talked about everything of importance to me.
When we were done He got up and went back to work
And I set out to enjoy His many blessings.

It's like this every day when I get up . . .
No matter how busy He is, or what He's doing
When I am ready I just call His name
And He drops what He's doing,
Comes down from on high
And spends time with me

ON EAGLES' WINGS

You let your days be filled with fears
And sleepless nights are spent with tears
Because you knew such awful pain
And swear to never walk again
Within that world, that living Hell
Or taste those tears you knew so well
You've built great fortress walls so high
Now, even Joy and Love deny
Because you fear you may invite
Those pains that haunt you in the night
You skirt the chance for Love's reward
While so much good in Life's ignored
Please, do not build your walls so high . . .
Come with me to where eagles fly
Let down your guard, release the gates . . .
Beyond those fortress walls Love waits
If you would let me dry your eyes
I'll take you where **my** spirit flies;
I'll lift you up, so far from fears
And you will have no time for tears
If you would only trust me to
I'll give Life's greatest joys to you
And never will you fear, or cry
Again
On eagles' wings your heart may fly

BEFORE YOU

Sometimes, when I think of you
Cold chills overtake me
And run up and down my spine
It's times like these
My eyes swell with tears
My breathing gets heavy
And I feel my whole world is beginning
Or ending
My thoughts of you
Bring such emotion
Bring such emotion
I laugh
I cry
All because of you
All because of you

Sometimes, when I think of you
I see my life pass before my eyes
And though I am thankful
For all that has made me what I am
I can't help feeling deep regret
That I ever loved another
Before you

That I ever wrote a love song
Before you
Before you
That I ever loved
Or ever wrote a love song
Before you
Before you

TOO BRIEFLY VISITED BY AN ANGEL

Once again, I must bear the pains
My life's Hell, where misery reigns
Days bring darkness and nights bring fears;
My life again engulfed with tears.
Again, I reached the heights of bliss
For I had felt an Angel's kiss
And known the joys true love can bring
But of these, briefly did I sing.
I loved that Angel so much more
Than all I'd ever loved before.
I gave my heart and soul to her
And of my love I was so sure.
In fact, so sure was I, I felt
My love, so hot, could make rocks melt!
I bet my life and all I'm worth
Upon this Angel sent to Earth
Who made me fly, who made me dance
Who kept me in a lover's trance.
But, only for one moment's span
In sweetest bliss we wreckless ran.
For, in an instant she was gone
And now my tears greet each day's dawn.
My hopes are dashed, my life's a hell
And pains return I've known so well.
How many times my heart has shed
Not blood, but bitter tears instead!
How many times must I bear pain?

How long such cruel misery reign?
Sometimes I think I can't go on . . .
What's the use? She'll still be gone.
Or, if I can, that I don't want to . . .
Life's so meaningless without you.
Will I make it through one more day?
Life is Hell, since you went away

A LITERAL LITANY
[Alliteral (sic) Litany]

Vast seas of sleeping trees still stand
Bleak and barren across the land.
While wrapped within white Winter's sleep
Past, unnoticed wee creatures creep
Crisp breeze briskly blasts through the trees
Still, hints of Spring this poet sees.
Though no green graces grass, or limb,
Or branch, no trace, however slim
Is seen, 't is buried just beneath
Cold, course bark, impervious sheath;
Tough shell that feigned cruel months so well.
Beneath, unseen, begins to swell
The essence of this Spring-to-be.
As Winter wanes, so soon you'll see
This land, but sleeping, did not die
While cold clouds crawled across the sky.
Just watch, and witness Nature's feat
Each marv'lous miracles a treat!

DEATH OF A SUN

You cannot know what you have done
But made my tears in rivers run.
Each day that comes without you near
I die, but first I shed a tear
For each and every little thing
I've lost, while, onto life I cling.
This song of sadness is the last
I'll ever sing; so quickly passed
Were things of joy or hopes I knew
That instant while I could love you.
Now dead, I find no will to be
Alive, and so, from life I flee.
I am now blazing like a sun
Once set in motion, death's begun.
I'm hurtling through my final arc
Though brilliant now, will soon be dark . . .
That life-supporting ray of light
Dead too, and disappears from sight.

Published in:
Tears of Fire
The National Library of Poetry, 1994

WINTER '95

Ev'rything goes quickly to sleep
Threats of frost daily creep
Those vibrant greens of Summer last
Yield to impending Winter blast
As yellow, red and brandy, plum
And orange, brown, and others come
Colors (all but green) are back once more
And all leaves turn and downward soar
To spread a blanket on the ground
Protecting plant life all around
So soon the trees are stripped and bare
For now, this barren shroud must wear
Now, many cold, harsh months we'll see
This look of death on every tree
And frozen winds will fill the skies
As this year's bitter North Wind cries

ANGEL

I sit in wonder and with praise
As God works mysterious ways
I'm awed by all that He has done
And by this Love that's now begun
Out of the blue did you appear
And Cupid's dart was like a spear
That struck me hard upon my chest
And I knew joys I'd never guessed
Could come to me or that I'd grow
In a short while to love you so
Despite my fears I gave my heart
And then with fervor did I start
To savor and to cherish bliss
That came in dreams of our first kiss
You are an Angel from above
And I am thankful for the love
That God has sent to see me through
This life, so much in love with you!

YOU AND ME

Your picture sits in front of me;
Your beauty's very plain to see.
Because you live so far away
I sit and dream of you today
And try to think what we would do
If I were here and I held you.
Our chance meeting, fast, fleeting;
That brief "hello," innocent greeting.
So long ago, we could not know
That love would blossom and would grow
And from a friendship we would be
So soon enraptured, you and me!
Such beauty flourished, swift and true;
So soon, so deeply, I loved you,
And, praise the Lord, you loved me!
Within such bliss were we set free,
For, who could know? Who might guess
Our misery and loneliness
So soon would wane and we might share
The sweetest love two hearts may dare?

SO MUCH I WANT TO SAY

There is so much I want to say
Upon this very special day
But words aren't easy now, I find
And can't express what's on my mind.
Of all the words that come to me
I hope that these will make you see
The depths of my great love for you;
This perfect love, though still quite new.
I know you understand my plight:
I've still no job and money's tight
So flowers, card, or fancy dress
I cannot give, but, nonetheless
These words are wrapped in pretty bows
A tribute to how my love grows.
In honor of your birthday, Dear
I pray these words will be quite clear
And touch your heart so you can be
On this day filled with joy and glee!

LIKE AN EAGLE

I told you I would write an ode
That would reflect my heart's abode.
Such feelings hidden deep inside
Evaded me each time I tried
To make them go into the form
That, in a poem is the norm.
But, this is meant to be so true
Of all the things I feel for you
And say the things that I now feel
And in this verse my love reveal.
In choosing words now as I write
(With lovely visions in my sight)
These meager words cannot express
The bliss I've known in your caress
Or love you've shown by ways you've cared
Or heights we've climbed by hopes we've dared.
So, though my words may not quite say
What keeps me in the clouds today
And makes my spirits soar so high
Or, like an eagle, makes me fly
I'll not give up, I'll search my mind
Until those words that I can find
Have said to you the best I dare
How much I love you, how I care.

CRY WITH ME

I'm glad to hear I've touched your heart
That in some way, within the art
Of poems written long ago
These simple words have moved you so

Another "Bright Star" cannot be
'T was written e'er you came to me
And though these words were said before
Within these lines I say much more

For, love I can now feel for you
Is crisper than the morning dew
And mountains high one cannot climb
No tranquil scenes are as sublime

No river, lake, or virgin pond
Or where the purest sky was dawned
No glimpse of Heaven I have seen
Or any lovely place I've been

No allegory, symbol of my mind
No matter how well thought's refined
Could ever find the words to say
What's in my heart for you today

For, you have touched that sacred part
Of me, you touched my lonely heart
And set me free from my distress
Now cradle me in your caress

No **"Bright Star"** can there be for you
But even better will I do
If you will let me I will try
To find the words to make you cry

So, cry with me in joy and bliss
As lips are joined and two souls kiss
And God's sweet Love can be revealed
And in our love His Love is sealed

LOST TO LOVE

The greatest task to face me yet:
To write those lines not written yet,
And say in words so you can see
The special things you've done for me.

If I had never loved before
Or into poems passions pour
These words might mean much more to you
And greater impact might come through.

But I have loved once on a time
And into words within a rhyme
Set down my thoughts and tried to do
In verse what I now try for you.

Thank God you understand my plight!
No matter how much, try I might,
To write in perfect verses here
I'll fail, no nearer perfect steer.

Still, trying will I never cease
As effort makes success increase
Until I've found the perfect lines
That glorify my heart's designs.

So, now, within this verse I send
The purest, deepest feelings penned
Of passions you now make me feel
And why within your love I reel.

My love increases day by day;
In flow'ry scented fields I lay,
Enraptured, wafting, lost to love
With thanks to loving God above

HEAVEN SENT

The early morning sun has come
And with it, rising, I am numb.
Though very tired, I could not sleep
And I awoke with that first peep
Of birds whose chorus grew so sweet
A melody with every tweet.

Because I know what this day brings
With joy, in verses, my heart sings
A prayer of thanks to God above
Who's blessed me with His perfect Love
And given me the greatest gifts,
As, in His Love my spirit drifts.

So, on my knees, I greet this day,
In waking seconds I must say
My thanks to Him for blessings sent
And for the bliss I know He meant
For me to feel because of you
And all the loving things you do.

Just knowing you traverse the miles
And soon will be here my heart smiles
And I am filled with so much joy
I dance and sing as little boy
Whose wonder and unbridled dreams
Overflows Elysian streams.

Without your love I could not see
These things that God has made for me
Or know the bliss that's Heaven sent
That marks this wonderous event
As, swiftly, to me you now race
And I am awed by our Lord's Grace!

MOVED TO CRY

It's overcast and threatens rain
This morning as I rack my brain
And search the cosmos for the way
To say what's in my heart today.
I want these words to be so right
And show the things within my sight
Just now, while visions of your face
Reveal to me God's Holy Grace.
No matter how hard, try I will
To choose the words, describe the thrill
Of feeling love that you now bring
Or why, with all my heart I sing,
I can but hope that they convey
Amazing things I want to say.
Amazing, yes, these things I feel,
With each new day does God reveal
His loving goodness and sweet gifts
He's planned for us and so uplifts
Our spirits to more Godly plane
And through His love will pleasure reign.
But, only by the Grace of God
And only with His loving nod
May we receive His blessings fine
Or feel these feelings so divine.

So, as I reach into my heart
And try, with words, within the art
Of poetry to glorify
My love for you I'm moved to cry
And cry with joy so all may see
What loving you has done for me!

I THANK GOD FOR THIS DAY

Just as this day dawns clear and bright
Sweet visions form in morning light
Enhanced by dew, made crisp and clean
Makes morning loveliest I've seen.
I greet this day with thanks and praise
To God, to Whom my hands I raise.
With love for me He made this day
And all He hoped was that I'd pray
A prayer of thanks in honor of
This day He made with so much love.
Because I know He made the sun
And morning's beauty's just begun,
The treasures of Creation shine,
His Masterpiece: this day's divine.
So as I pray, I offer thanks
For trees and birds and river banks;
For hills and dales and rolling grain
And wind through branches sweet refrain.
I offer praise for all He made,
For things in sunlight and in shade.
Each place I look I see His might,
So humbly marvel at the sight
Of all the things today displays
And my sweet Lord I gladly praise!

FIFTY YEARS OF LOVE

So long ago, in times gone by
As one you vowed your love to try.
In trying thus, in love you stayed
And, one by one, we each were made
A bit of Mom, a bit of Dad;
No greater parents kids have had.

Upon this very special day
Your sons and daughters all will say
A prayer of thanks to God above
Who blessed us with the greatest love
That two dear parents could bestow
For such a love a child should know.

Without your love we could not be
Alive, nor live in ecstasy
For all the love that we have known
As, older, each of us has grown.
And, as years came and as they went
We're thankful for each moment spent.

No greater parents ever known,
Nor truer love at home was shown.
Your love for us, so strong and true,
Has made us feel this love for you
And love we feel now brings us tears;
Our love for you lasts through the years.

Now, fifty years of wedded bliss
Commemorated in the kiss
We each now place upon your cheek
We honor love all children seek
And we express our love for you,
For love you give by all you do.

These meager words are meant to say
The feelings felt by us today
In celebrating fifty years;
Your wedded bliss, the hopes, the tears,
But, most of all, the most sublime:
The love we've talked of in this rhyme.

With our love
and
best wishes
on your
Fiftieth Wedding Anniversary
December 25th, 1998

 BONUS SECTION

PERFECT COUPLETS

Seventy seven rhymed couplets, having "perfect"
measure (line length), extracted from all the poems I have
written between April, 1966 and September, 1996]

23 characters

So I just walked around
My eyes upon the ground

For writing Epic Poetry
Just call upon Calliope

24 characters

Summer Falls into Winter
Then Springs into Summer

28 characters

So I can give my love to you
And we can do what lovers do

I cannot help myself and now
In pieces fall my broken vow

29 characters

Just now, I can but reminisce
Remembering that deepest kiss

30 characters

But I am shocked at what I see
What I'm seeing just cannot be

From far away, out of the blue
Our unexpected friendship grew

The only thing I need for life
I have: you are my loving wife

I adore her, love kept growing
Passions kindled, ever glowing

I'd sailed upon the seven seas
And tasted every briney breeze
That rushed upon a distant shore
Or through a coral reef did roar

31 characters

Melodic voices, pleasing, sweet
Uplifting, sit at Father's feet

Clio helps write historic facts
While Thalia, with comedic acts

And, pausing once again to rest
Upon the far-off mountain crest

So lovingly, I'll hold you near
And always cherish you, my Dear

Within your arms I long to live
And no one else my love to give

For half a day this golden ball
Will rise and to its apex crawl

Because I know how great God is
I know your love, a gift of His

Two bows of ribbon in your hair
One for color and one for flair

In the endless search for peace
Man renews his next war's lease

I just cherish each sweet minute
Of your grace and live within it

And burning, craving you so much
Longing, yearning for your touch

There are so many days like this
Sometimes the sunny ones we miss

I long to hold you in these ways
And lay with you for all my days

We haven't known each other long
But two hearts sing a happy song

Immortal, fine, my words will be
When Muses choose to sit with me

To me, so rare and pure, so fine
I'll always cherish; it's divine

As color hangs as emerald drapes
Upon the branches Nature's capes

In Nineteen-Sixty-Nine your face
Upon my mind last left its trace

Beyond my reach, beyond my touch
I'm sad, and missing you so much

33 characters

The Tourist gone, for good reason
He cannot stand the Winter Season

Once again, I must bear the pains
Life's a Hell where misery reigns

That night, alone, in our own way
Our eyes begged the other to stay

As daylight fades and color pales
Cold winds arrive in bitter gales

So, as I sit and write this rhyme
And up to greater heights I climb

For many years were dreams denied
And silent, bitter tears we cried

I cannot help, but think of bliss
That comes within your sweet kiss

Just now, I cherish every thought
Of every feeling you have brought

In such a way, through fellowship
My loving God breaks Satan's grip

I lay so close, right next to you
And dream what I would love to do
If you awoke and saw me there
Playing gently with your hair

34 characters

Entranced by wonders out in space
Each one's a feature of your face
Where Beauty reigns, a happy queen
And you're that beauty I have seen

I have now waited these long weeks
Denied the pleasures my love seeks

Since first you came into my space
I was entranced by your sweet face

We always share the greatest bliss
In greatest passion's rapture kiss

But, now, as e'er we two must face
Between us comes this little space

It rumbles o'er these wooded hills
And with great joy my spirit fills

Last night we met and now I'm free
The love I've sought I can now see

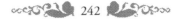

I start and end each day like this
No chance to pray will I dare miss

35 characters

Though verse and rhyme I may employ
They can't describe the perfect joy

I'll lift you up, so far from fears
And you will have no time for tears

You may not know what you have done
But kindled flames as would the sun

But rain is good and as this squall
Relieves itself those droplets fall

For, soon, you will be home with me
And passions of our dreams set free

I've written lots of verse in rhyme
And measured metric thought sublime

Despite five-thousand miles between
Two souls, a love as n'er was seen

So, when I'm blessed to sit on high
With Muses, while, with verse I try

While we both felt within our souls
Our lives were not fulfilling goals

36 characters

That friendship was a precious thing
And our two hearts as one would sing

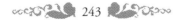 243

So, we won't mind when droplets fall
We'll grab our boots and have a ball

I would think this should not matter
Surely, not this whole Earth shatter

But, first the rolling thunder comes
And pounds the air like kettle drums

Young and fair, through eons singing
Revealing hope the future's bringing

You are my greatest dreams come true
I'll always have sweet dreams of you

37 characters

Thus, with the simple words you trace
You help to show the world God's face

The rush and noise, this frantic life
All of the trials, trouble and strife

Though one more year is soon to close
My love for you still grows and grows

At first, small buttons dot the trees
Then, foliage sways within the breeze

38 characters
With joy I drift midst thoughts of you
All things seem sweet with morning dew

Below, though all the life has browned
Above, with brilliant diamonds crowned

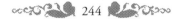

I'd been where snowdrifts pile so high
Where ageless treetops touched the sky

You called last night and filled me in
On what you'd done and how you've been

Let down your guard, release the gates
Beyond these fortress walls Love waits

39 characters
Soon born of hopes and dreams has grown
And now our hearts this Love have known

42 characters

White peaks pierce clouds where eagles soar
While deep through canyons North Winds roar

Ross Edward Percifield, II
Copyright February 15, 1997

BOOKS BY ROSS EDWARD PERCIFIELD, II

Synopses from
The Amazing Adventures Of Alderon
An Epic Journey In Verse

Now, you may travel to the land of Indium, that beautiful and magical place of long ago and far away and be with our Hero, Alderon the Bold, as he pursues many exciting adventures and quests.

Synopses . . . Books I – V

In **Book I – Quest For Indium**, you will meet Alderon, born to loving parents, who, as a youth learns the art and skill of warfare fighting for many Kings and Queens in lands far from his home. Soon a strong young man, our Hero returns to Indium after seven years to learn the awful news: the evil Lord Kallus has raised an army and made a cruel assault on the castle. You will be there, through tragedy and triumph, as Alderon attempts to regain his home.

Book II – In The Dragons' Lair, is all about dragons. You will meet the four brothers: Krag, Dag, Daug and Kak, fierce fire-breathing dragons grown thirsty for the taste of man's blood once again, and you will be there when they begin to wreak great terror in Indium. You will be there when our brave Hero trades his own life for his people's, and you will fly with him when he is carried off, a prisoner, to the dragons' high mountain lair. You will also meet the mighty Eagle-King and see how he plays a very important part in the end of this chapter.

In **Book III – <u>Wizards And A Wife</u>**, you will learn of the lustful but cowardly wizard Kel-Dor, who, using the ancient craft conjures up a blood-thirsty Beast Man and commands this wicked monster with his army to make a fierce attack on Castle Indium. You will witness the awful battle, and its outcome, and you will be there by Rivers Ardain and Keil when Alderon meets the fair maiden, Grace, and experiences such deep feelings he's never known before.

Book IV – A Friend In Need, begins again in peaceful Indium and you are there on the day when Alderon's first child is born and you will share his joy. But, soon that peaceful, happy time is ended, when Alderon receives an urgent plea for help from his old friend King Elric, III of Mendomain, besieged by the greedy Kur and his cutthroat band of mercenaries. Can he get there in time? Can he help save his friend? You will once again see great battles and learn the answers to these questions, and you will see a side of Alderon you never knew existed.

As **Book V – Flames In Indium** opens, Alderon and his army make the long trip home from Mendomain and as they sing songs telling of their many adventures they are filled with a mixture of emotions, having slain Kur and defeating his army but not being able to get there in time to prevent King Elric, III from being viciously slain by Kur's own sword.

True happiness was to be felt, though, when the weary men returned to their beloved Castle Indium and this was true more so for Alderon, for, on their arrival he was astounded to learn that prior to their departure, his loving wife Grace had become pregnant and he was now the proud father of a beautiful son named Bastion.

There were great celebrations and peaceful times returned to Indium. In the next several peaceful years, Alderon and Grace ruled their Kingdom well and spent much time schooling Destiny and Bastion in the arts of ruling a kingdom, as well as teaching them the skills needed to command and lead an army.

It was after this time then, a vicious horde of dragons grew bold and hungry for the taste of Man and made a fierce assault on Indium. These beasts were not as large, nor could they speak as the four brother dragons you learned about in Book II. But their might was great for the sky was darkened as hundreds flew forth. Many brave men perished, their wives and children too, and many heroes made; such desperate fighting on those days. Yes, Alderon and his brave men fought nobly, but it was on the fifth day when a brave and mighty Eagle King who had rescued Alderon at the end of Book II returned to offer help once more.

Yes, the Eagle King and great numbers of his comrades flew down and soon the tide of battle was finally turned. After much vicious fighting and with corpses of men and dragons laying everywhere the battle was finished and the last surviving beasts flew beyond the horizon.

As this Book ends, peace is restored again in Indium, castle Indium is cleansed of all traces of the attack, and at a special Holiday decreed by Alderon all of the brave and faithful men who helped in the fight were gifted a chest of gold and the Eagle King is freed from the curse put on him long ago and he is restored to Jan the Elder, King of Ta Rand.

As this is being written, Book VI is in production and has yet to be titled. Book VI will take you on more great adventures and quests in the continuing epic journey. Each Book is composed in four metric feet (eight syllables) per line and set down in "iambic" rhymed couplets in four line stanzas. As a "Bonus," each and every of the 260 rhymed couplets in Book I are what the Author calls "Perfect Couplets," each line having the same line length, i.e., the same number of characters, spaces and punctuation (excluding ending punctuation,) as its rhyming mate. In fact, of the 130 four line stanzas in Book I, twenty one (over one sixth!) qualify as "Perfect Stanzas," as:

Lines 41-44

As good time shone upon the land 32

King Eldon claimed Lysea Grahnde 32

To be his queen and in their joy 32
They soon conceived a little boy 32

Lines 53-56
Thus, Alderon, who would be king 32
A source of songs the Poets sing 32
So soon would be a strapping lad 32
And he such great adventures had 32

Lines 57-60
Exploring distant realms he went 32
As time in far-off land he spent 32
Where icy mountains poke the sky 32
While fire-breathing dragons fly 32

Lines 321-324
Because that fortress is so high 32
With towers reaching to blue sky 32
From walls of castle very strong 32
The battle will be hard and long 32

Lines 365-368
As Kallus' dead were buried then 32
And army's quivers stocked again 32
Sporadic shooting here and there 32
Of flaming arrows filled the air. 32

In the tradition and style of Homer, Milton, and others of classical romantic poetry, this Poet presents his inspired telling of **The Amazing Adventures Of Alderon**. While the structure of the verse is quite rigid, its melodic and lyrical quality allows it to be easily read. As much as this work is a Poem, it is a Song, for, every poem is a song, and every song a poem. Come now, as this Poet sings this song for you. <u>ero, Alderon the Bold, Hero, AlderonHero</u>

Printed in the United States
By Bookmasters